Choose your Words

A School Thesaurus

Choose Your Words

A School Thesaurus

by

C. Windridge

Allied Publishing Group, Inc. 2003

Printed in Canada

Contents

Preface

A Student's First Thesaurus is a handy thesaurus for all students between 9 and 13 years of age. It provides for many of the important and immediate language needs of these students and is designed to become their invaluable companion. The students' attention should first be directed to the notes 'How to use this thesaurus' (page vii).

The book consists of a basic list of over two thousand commonly-used guide words (pages 9 to 115), carefully selected and arranged in alphabetical order. Alongside each guide word there is a group of synonyms and words that are similar in meaning. Occasionally, these groups contain words that have only a tenuous similarity in meaning to the relevant guide word, but may provide preferable alternatives: to this extent the author has used his considerable teaching experience to anticipate some of the errors frequently made by students. By using this section of the book, students will enlarge and enrich their vocabulary. It follows that they will develop their ability to speak or write more accurately or more stylishly and so express themselves more effectively.

The basic list of guide words is followed by a supplement which contains alphabetical lists of 'opposites' (pages 116 to 139)—some are true antonyms and some are approximately opposite in meaning but useful for the students to know and use. There are also separate pages of commonly-used archaic words (page 141) that the pupil will discover in literature and frequently-used foreign words and phrases (pages 142 and 143). The supplement also contains a set of simple instructions to assist the formation of antonyms by using the appropriate affixes (page 140). Taken together, the words in the basic list and the words in the supplement provide the student with a wide choice from close to 20,000 words.

How to use this thesaurus

Please read the following notes carefully.

What is a thesaurus?

A thesaurus has the appearance and some of the qualities of a dictionary and it can be used as such on a limited scale. However, the essential difference between a dictionary and a thesaurus is this: in a dictionary you refer to words whose meanings are not known to you, or about which you are uncertain, and so become fully acquainted with their correct meanings, whereas in a thesaurus you refer to familiar words, whose meanings are already known to you, and thereby become aware of less familiar words with the same or similar meanings but which may be more suitable for your purpose.

Guide words

The first column contains an alphabetical list, in bold type, of many of the everyday words with which you should be familiar. These are the *guide words.* They are the words to which you refer. Guide words that are spelled the same but differ in meaning with pronunciation are dealt with as follows:

content *a.* happy, pleased, glad, satisfied
content *n.* filling, constituents, ingredients, capacity, volume

The underlining indicates the stressed syllable(s).

In general, only one part of speech is shown, e.g., **absent** (page 10), is shown as an adjective although it is also a verb. Exceptionally, more than one part of speech is shown where there is likely to be confusion or where the various parts of speech have different meanings, e.g., **abandon, abandoned** (page 9). If the word you have in mind is not listed in the guide words, then refer to another common word of the same meaning, e.g., **misuse** is not in the guide words, but *misuse* and the words of a similar meaning are to be found alongside **abuse** (page 10).

Abbreviations

The second column contains the abbreviations that are used to indicate the parts of speech. These abbreviations, which are in italics, are as follows:

a. adjective *adv.* adverb *conj.* conjunction *int.* interjection
n. noun *prep.* preposition *pron.* pronoun *v.* verb.

Synonyms and words of similar meaning

The third column contains *synonyms* (words that are identical in meaning), words that are similar in meaning and words that are only approximately similar in meaning. From these, you select the most suitable word for your purpose and, generally, this means the word that is the most accurate or the most stylish.

You must exercise great caution when selecting words, for words of a similar meaning cannot always be freely interchanged, e.g., **abolish** (page 9) is similar in meaning to *invalidate,* but *abolished* cannot be replaced by *invalidated* in this sentence: "Lincoln *abolished* slavery."

Quite often, a word that is only approximately similar in meaning to the guide word is the best alternative, e.g., *frequent* is not a synonym of **visit** (page 109), but *frequented* is preferable to *visited* in this sentence: "They *visited* a café." One assumes "visited a café" is intended to mean "visited a café quite often" and not "visited a café on one occasion only."

Some guide words have more than one meaning. In these cases, the words that follow the guide word are separately listed, and the lists are numbered, e.g., **abreast** (page 9).

Alternative spellings and additional information are given in parentheses, e.g.,

abduct *v.* . . . steal (a child) (page 9).

A specimen sentence is provided where there is likely to be some doubt about the use of a word, e.g., **above** *a.* The **above** statement is correct (page 9).

The symbol / is used to save space and avoid repetition, e.g., **aboveboard** (page 9) means "without suspicion." It also means "without deceit" and "without deception." These alternatives are given as "without suspicion/deceit/deception."

Supplement

This section (pages 116 to 143) contains lists of *antonyms* (words that are directly opposite in meaning) and words that are almost opposite in meaning (pages 116 to 139), archaic words (page 141), and foreign words and phrases (pages 142 and 143).

Where a guide word is more than one part of speech or has more than one meaning, its opposites are separately listed, and the lists are numbered, e.g., **abandon** 1. keep, retain, hold, remain in, occupy, take over; 2. restraint, caution, care.

The section **Forming Opposites** (page 140) shows you how to form opposites, or antonyms, by using suitable affixes.

A a

aback *adv.* backward, backwards, to the back, rearward, rearwards, to the rear, in reverse, behind
taken aback: *surprised, amazed, astonished, astounded, shocked*

abandon *v.* give up, surrender, yield, relinquish, disown, leave, depart from, quit, resign, desert, forsake, vacate
n. freedom, liberty, no restraint, excitement, rashness, recklessness, carelessness, impulsiveness, lust, licentiousness

abandoned *a.* 1. given up, surrendered, relinquished, disowned, derelict, deserted, forsaken, vacated, vacant, unoccupied, empty
2. unrestrained, reckless, rash, wanton, lustful, licentious, carefree

abate *v.* decrease, reduce, diminish, lessen, weaken, quiet, cease, end, finish, terminate

abdomen *n.* belly, bowels, intestines

abduct *v.* kidnap, carry off by force, take away, remove (a person), steal (a child)

abhor *v.* hate, detest, loathe, dislike intensely, regard with disgust/distaste

abide *v.* 1. dwell, stay, live, reside, lodge, rest, remain, wait
2. suffer, put up with, submit to, bear, endure, stand, tolerate, accept

ability *n.* skill, talent, cleverness, smartness, competence, capability, ingenuity, capacity, power

able *a.* skillful, talented, clever, smart, competent, efficient, capable, ingenious

abnormal *a.* unusual, odd, strange, eccentric, queer, peculiar, bizarre, irregular, uncommon, extraordinary, exceptional

aboard *prep.* on, on to, on board, in, into, inside

abolish *v.* do away with, end, finish, terminate, destroy, quash, invalidate, disallow, ban, bar, make void, annul, nullify, eliminate, remove

abound *v.* be rich in/in excess/infested with/plentiful/well-stocked, teem, overflow

about *prep.* of, to do with, concerned with, in regard to, in connection with, relative to, in relation to
adv. round, around, all round, approximately, nearly, almost

above *prep.* over, higher than, on top of, superior to
adv. overhead, on high, upstairs, The sun is **above** us.
a. The **above** statement is correct.

aboveboard *a.* fair, honest, just, true, right, correct, proper, upright, straight, straightforward, sound, without suspicion/deceit/deception, open, undisguised

abreast *a.* 1. side by side
They walked two or three **abreast.**
2. up to date with, in touch with, aware.
Do you keep **abreast** of the times?

abroad *adv.* far away, in/to a foreign land/another distant country

abrupt *a.* sudden, unexpected, violent, sharp, quick, hurried, hasty, short, precipitate, blunt, curt, cross, brusque, terse, tart, laconic

absent *a.* away, not in existence/present/here, lacking, abstracted in mind

absentminded *a.* inattentive, forgetful, unmindful, heedless, dreamy, not alert/vigilant/watchful, careless, unwary

absolute *a.* 1. complete, full, utmost
2. without limit, unrestricted, perfect, real, true, great, pure, unlimited, independent, arbitrary

absorb *v.* take/suck in, soak/swallow, up, engross
He was **absorbed** in a book.

abstain *v.* refrain, avoid, not take part in/participate

abstract *a.* unreal, impractical, ideal, vague, abstruse, theoretical
n. summary, brief list, short account, essence
v. remove, take away, steal, disengage, separate, deduct, condense, summarize, shorten

absurd *a.* silly, ridiculous, foolish, puerile, not sensible, nonsensical, crazy, stupid, asinine, brainless, odd, strange, eccentric, preposterous, unreasonable, irrational, illogical

abundance *n.* plenty, wealth, riches, overflow, excess, large/ample stock/supply, generous amount, spate, proliferation

abundant *a.* plentiful, rich, in excess, overflowing, teeming, rank, luxuriant, pouring, prolific, well-stocked, copious, ample, substantial, adequate, generous, considerable, boundless, unrestricted, unlimited

abuse *v.* use wrongly, misuse, harm, damage, injure, mistreat, maltreat, ill-treat, treat badly
n. Litter is an **abuse** of the countryside.
a. *"You idiot"* are **abusive** words.

accelerate *v.* increase speed/motion/velocity/rate, move/go faster/quicker/swifter/more rapidly, speed up

accept *v.* take, receive, undertake, abide by, tolerate, agree to/with, allow, regard favorably, approve, believe

access *n.* way in, entrance, doorway, door, passage, channel, opening, inlet, ingress, approach

accident *n.* 1. mishap, misfortune, ill fortune, unfortunate, occurrence, injury, calamity
2. unexpected event, unpredictable occurrence, chance

accommodate *v.* 1. oblige, serve, suit, provide for, equip, supply, furnish
2. house, lodge, provide rooms/dwelling/home/shelter/quarters for

accompany *v.* go with, escort, guide, be a companion to, assist, help, aid, support

accomplice *n.* partner/helper/assistant in wrongdoing/crime, accessory

accomplish *v.* do, achieve, perform, manage, succeed in doing

account *n.* 1. report, story, description
2. invoice, bill, financial statement/record
3. reason, cause, explanation
v. give reason, find cause, explain, be responsible

accumulate *v.* gather, collect, assemble, amass, save, hoard, store

accurate *a.* exact, precise, correct, true, truthful, honest, reliable, dependable

accuse *v.* blame, charge, put/lay blame/responsibility on, indict

achieve *v.* gain, win, get, obtain, acquire, attain, reach, carry out, perform, accomplish

acid *a.* acidic, vinegary, tart, sour, harsh, biting, severe, sharp

acknowledge *v.* admit, recognize, take notice of, accept, confess, declare, grant, own, allow, answer, greet, salute

acquaint *v.* make known to/aware of, inform of/about

acquire *v.* gain, obtain, get, receive, win, come to own/possess, take, annex, collect, glean, achieve, attain, procure

act *n.*
1. deed, feat, accomplishment
2. part (of a stage play), performance

v.
1. do, perform, behave, work, operate
2. pretend, sham, feign, mimic, mime, simulate, deceive, be false

action *n.*
1. act, deed, performance
2. activity, movement, motion, work
3. battle, conflict Soldiers die in **action.**

active *a.* quick-moving, quick, rapid, fast, swift, lively, alive, brisk, spry, sprightly, nimble, agile, vivacious, busy, industrious, hard-working, energetic, vigorous, effective

actual *a.* real, true, genuine, present, current, existing, established

acute *a.*
1. sharp, pointed, not blunt An angle which contains less than 90° is **acute**.
2. high, penetrating, shrill
3. keen, sensitive, sharp, quick
4. severe, serious, critical, intense

adamant *a.* stubborn, firm, determined, unyielding, resolute, obdurate

adapt *v.* adjust, change, alter, fit, suit, remodel, modify The film was **adapted** from the novel.

address *n.*
1. place, location
2. talk, speech, oration, discourse

v.
1. I shall **address** the envelope.
2. give a talk to, make a speech to, orate/hold forth to, harangue

adequate *a.* sufficient, enough, ample, suitable, satisfactory, fit, proper

adhere *v.* stick, stick together, cling, attach

adhesive *n.* gum, glue, paste, cement, fixative, sticky substance, mucilage

a. Gum and molasses are **adhesive**.

adjacent *a.* next, side by side, alongside, near, near by, close, neighboring

adjust *v.* change, alter, adapt, arrange, regulate

admire *v.* respect, approve, like, appreciate, esteem, praise, applaud

admission *n.* admittance, entrance, access

admit *v.* accept, allow, grant, confess, declare, recognize, acknowledge

adopt *v.* choose, select, take, take over, accept

adore *v.* love, cherish, worship, admire, intensely, deify

adrift *adv.* drifting, untied, unmoored, free

adult *a.* mature, grown-up, fully-grown

advance *v.* 1. progress, go forward, approach
2. offer, propose, make an overture
She **advanced** a few hints.
3. lend, pay cash/money in advance
He advanced her $14.50.

advantage *n.* 1. help, aid, benefit, profit, gain
2. superiority, better position
take advantage: *act unfairly*

adversary *n.* enemy, foe, opponent, rival, antagonist, contestant

advertise *v.* make known, make public, publicize

advice *n.* counsel, guidance, opinion given, news, information, notification, bulletin

affair *n.* matter, business, concern, event, occasion, incident

affect *v.* 1. change, move, touch (emotionally)
2. pretend, act, assume, practice
a. The actress is vain and **affected**.

affection *n.* love, liking, fondness, tenderness, attachment, endearment

afford *v.* 1. be able/have the means/be wealthy enough to buy/purchase, spare
2. supply, provide, give, furnish, bestow, yield

aflame *a.* in flame, flaming, alight, on fire, afire, aglow, glowing, ablaze, blazing, burning

afloat *adv.* floating, at sea, aboard ship, on board ship

afraid *a.* frightened, scared, alarmed, in fear, fearful, timid, uneasy, apprehensive

age *n.* 1. long time, era, period
2. later life
v. grow/become older, develop

agent *n.* 1. representative, deputy, steward, factor
2. force, cause, means

aggressive *a.* quarrelsome, belligerent, bellicose, warlike

agile *a.* nimble, lively, spry, athletic, active, quick-moving, brisk

agitate *v.* 1. bother, disturb, excite, alarm, worry, fluster
2. stir, shake, move

agony *n.* great pain, anguish, torment, suffering

agree *v.* 1. concur, approve, allow, accept, grant, share opinion, consent, concede
2. match, correspond, coincide

agreeable *a.* pleasant, pleasing, tasteful, inviting, well-disposed, satisfactory, willing/ready/prepared to accept, acceptable, in agreement

agreement *n.* 1. promise, bargain, contract, bond, guarantee, warranty, covenant, treaty, truce, pact, pledge
2. accord, concord, mutual understanding

ahead *adv.* in advance, in front, before, forward

aid *n.* help, assistance, support
v. help, assist, succor, support

ailment *n.* illness, sickness, malady

aim *n.* purpose, intent, intention, object, objective, target, goal, ambition, end
v. 1. intend, resolve
2. take aim/a line on, direct, level, point (at a target)

air *n.* 1. atmosphere
2. appearance, manner, style
v. dry, warm, allow air to enter (room/clothes)

alarm *n.* 1. warning, alert
2. fear, fright, panic, excitement, agitation
v. 1. warn, alert, make aware
2. frighten, disturb, startle, excite, agitate

alert *a.* lively, alive, active, nimble, spry, attentive, wide-awake, wary, cautious, watchful, vigilant
n. alarm, warning
v. alarm, warn, make aware

alight *a.* lighted, on fire, burning, aflame, in flame
v. get down, descend, dismount, settle

alike *a.* like, similar, akin
adv. similarly, in like matter

allow *v.* 1. let, permit, consent/agree to, tolerate, accept, abide by, put up with, stand, suffer, bear, award, give, grant, bestow
2. admit, own, agree, concede, concur, confess, declare, acknowledge, recognize

almost *adv.* nearly, all but

aloft *adv.* above, overhead, high up, upward

alone *a.* lone, lonely, solitary
adv. only, exclusively

also *adv.* too, besides, in addition, additionally, as well, furthermore, moreover, what is more

alter *v.* change, vary, modify, adjust, rearrange, remodel, redesign, adapt, convert, transform

altogether *adv.* entirely, wholly, on the whole, totally, in total, completely, fully

amateur *n.* beginner, novice, nonprofessional

amaze *v.* surprise, astonish, astound, fill with wonder, overwhelm, shock, flabbergast, dumbfound

ambition *n.* desire, hope, aspiration, aim, target, goal, object, objective

amend *v.* correct, put right, make better, better, reform, improve

amiable *a.* friendly, agreeable, amicable, good-natured, well-disposed, of good humor, good-tempered, even-tempered, pleasant, likeable, lovable

among *prep.* amongst, amid, amidst

amount *n.* 1. quality, number, total
2. cost, total cost, full value
v. The bill **amounts** to $8.96.

ample *a.* enough sufficient, adequate, more than enough, generous, substantial, abundant, plentiful, rich, copious

amuse *v.* entertain, cause laughter, make laugh, be comical/funny, divert, entertain, beguile

anger *n.* rage, annoyance, wrath, ire, temper, vexation, fury, irritation

angle *n.* 1. corner, sharp, bend/turn, point
2. approach, aspect, slant, viewpoint, standpoint

animal *n.* beast, brute, creature
animals: *creatures, animal-life, fauna*

announce *v.* make known, tell, declare, report, reveal, advertise, broadcast, proclaim, publish, notify

annoy *v.* anger, enrage, exasperate, harass, aggravate, irritate, bother, pester, molest, badger

annual *a.* yearly
n. A marigold plant is an **annual**.

anonymous *a.* nameless, unknown

another *a.* one more, a different, an additional
pron. additional one

answer *n.* 1. solution, result
2. reply, retort

anticipate *v.* expect, hope, predict, forestall, use in advance, look forward to, realize/consider beforehand, accelerate

anxiety *n.* worry, concern, disquiet, uneasiness, trouble, anguish

apart *adv.* aside, separately, independently, asunder
set apart: *put aside/on one side, reserve, devote*

apparel *n.* dress, clothing, attire, garments, garb

apparent *a.* seen, clear, plain, obvious, probable, likely

appeal *v.* request, beg, ask, pray, plead, entreat, implore, beseech

appear *v.* 1. become apparent/visible, come into sight/view, materialize
2. look, seem

applaud *v.* praise, laud, clap hands, cheer, shout for, acclaim, commend

apply *v.* 1. ask, request, make an application
2. attend, commit, devote, engage

appreciation *n.* 1. estimation, judgement, understanding, perception, recognition, approval, admiration
2. rise/growth/increase in value

approach *n.* 1. way to/in, access, entrance
2. advance, overture, offer, proposal
v. near, go closer to, come towards

appropriate *a.* correct, right, proper, suitable, becoming, fit, fitting, befitting, apt, apposite, well put/said/chosen, relevant, adequate

appropri<u>ate</u> *v.* take possession of, steal, annex, confiscate

approve *v.* accept, like, esteem, allow, permit, sanction, assent/consent to, agree to/with, confirm, commend

apt *a.* 1. suitable, appropriate, fit, fitting, befitting, becoming
2. witty, quick-witted, smart, clever, apposite, well put/chosen (remark)

argue *v.* differ, dispute, discuss, debate, prove, reason, maintain, indicate

arms *n.* 1. weapons
2. upper limbs (of humans), branches, outgrowths, projections, crosspieces

aroma *n.* sweet smell/scent/odor/essence, perfume, fragrance

arouse *v.* awaken, waken, rouse, bestir, stir into action/activity, stimulate

arrange *v.* 1. order, group, sort, select, adjust
2. plan, prepare, organize

arrest *v.* 1. stop, halt, check, apprehend
2. catch, hold, grasp, take prisoner, secure, capture, seize

art *n.* skill, craft, technique, knack, trade, aesthetic activity

artful *a.* cunning, crafty, sly, wily, deceitful, devious

article *n.* 1. object, item, thing, ware
2. account, description, extract

ascend *v.* rise, go/get/come up, scale, slope upwards

ashamed *a.* abashed, guilt-conscious, aware of disgrace, embarrassed

ask *v.* 1. request, invite, call for, demand, require, want, need
2. inquire, question, call for an answer
ask after: *inquire about (a person)*

assault *n.* violent attack/advance, onslaught, charge, rape

assemble *v.* 1. fit/put/join together, build, construct, erect, compile, combine
2. gather, together, congregate, collect, meet, convene, throng, group, muster, rally

assist *v.* help, aid, succor, support

associate *v.* join, join together/in mix, partner, affiliate, relate to

assortment *n.* mixture, collection, variety, selection

assume *v.* suppose, pretend, act, simulate, take for granted, take upon, undertake

assure *v.* convince, give confidence to, guarantee, make sure/safe/certain, tell with confidence

astonish *v.* astound, surprise, amaze, shock, overwhelm, fill with wonder, flabbergast, dumbfound

astound *v.* astonish, surprise, amaze, shock, overwhelm, make wonder, flabbergast, dumbfound

astray *adv.* off course, wandering, out of the way
gone astray: *lost, mislaid*

attach *v.* fasten, fix, affix, connect, combine, join, unite, bind, marry, tie

attachment *n.* bond, devotion, friendship, affection, love, fondness, endearment

attack *n.* 1. bout, spell, turn, fit, spasm, sudden occurrence
2. assault, onslaught, battle
v. assault, fall upon, do battle with, storm charge

attain *v.* achieve, accomplish, gain, get, obtain, win, earn, reach, arrive at, come to

attempt *n.* try, trial, endeavor, essay

attend *v.* 1. be present at, go regularly to
2. escort guide, accompany, serve, wait upon, help, assist, aid support
3. heed, take notice, give thought/attention/care/consideration/application, show interest

attire *n.* dress, clothing, apparel, garments, garb, costume

attract *v.* draw to/towards, bring near, influence, please, excite, entice, lure, charm

audacity *n.* boldness, forwardness, pertness, sauciness, cheek, impudence, impertinence

audience *n.* 1. listeners, spectators, assembly, gathering
2. interview, hearing

authentic *a.* real, true, genuine, of undoubted origin, trustworthy, reliable

authority *n.* power, right, rule, control, command, influence, administration, government

avail *v.* help, be of value/profit, benefit

available *a.* near, handy, within reach, on supply, supplied

avarice *n.* greed, love of wealth/riches/possessions, possessiveness

average *a.* normal, usual, standard, common, ordinary, medium, mean, mediocre

aversion *n.* dislike, distaste, antipathy, loathing, abhorrence

avert *v.* avoid, prevent, ward off, turn away

avoid *v.* escape, avert, shun, dodge, refrain/abstain/keep away from, elude

await *v.* wait for, expect, anticipate, be kept for
A letter and a parcel **await** you.

awake *v.* awaken, wake, wake up, arouse, rouse, rouse up, bestir

aware *a.* conscious, knowing, cognizant, well-informed, wary, watchful, vigilant, wide-awake, mindful

away *adv.* 1. at/to a distance, another place, off, aside, apart, absent, not present
2. constantly, continuously, on and on, all the time
The gardener works **away** with his spade

awe *n.* wonder, respect, reverence, fear

awkward *a.* clumsy, bungling, unskillful, gawky, ungainly, ill-adapted, difficult, not easy, risky, embarrassing

B b

babble *v.* prattle, gab, gabble, jabber, gibber, chatter, speak unintelligibly/confusedly/excessively/foolishly/babyishly, be inarticulate/incoherent, talk idly
n. prattle, idle talk, babytalk

babyish *a.* infantile, childish, immature, silly

back *n.* rear, hinder part, reverse side
v. 1. support, assist, help
2. go back/backwards, reverse
3. bet/gamble/wager/stake on

backward *a.* 1. slow, behindhand, retarded, dull, unintelligent, obtuse, reluctant, reticent, shy
2. reversed, in reverse
adv. backwards, rearward, rearwards, behind, aback

bad *a.* 1. naughty, badly-behaved, unruly, disobedient, ill-mannered, rude, wrong, evil, malevolent, immoral, vile, sinful, vicious, vindictive, malignant, corrupt, depraved, base, lustful, profligate, licentious
2. poor, lacking in quality, faulty, defective, blemished, unpleasant, distasteful, noxious, harmful, debased, tainted, unwholesome, adulterated, decayed, rotten, putrefied
3. ill, sick, ailing, not well, unwell, poorly, indisposed

badge *n.* mark, sign, symbol, emblem, device, token, crest

badger *v.* bully, browbeat, threaten, worry, bother, tease, torment, persecute

baffle *v.* mystify, bewilder, perplex, hoax, puzzle, confuse, confound, deceive, mislead, elude, hinder

baggage *n.* bags, cases, luggage, belongings

bait *v.* worry, bother, trouble, anger, annoy, browbeat, heckle, tease, torment, cause to bite
n. lure (in a trap or on a fish-hook), enticement

balance *v.* weigh, make equal, equate, match, equalize, keep in equilibrium, counterpoise, neutralize, waver, oscillate
n. 1. poise, equilibrium, neutrality
2. scales, weighing-machine

ball *n.* 1. sphere, spheroid, globe, globule, orb, shot
2. dance, social gathering

ban *v.* forbid, bar, not permit/allow, disallow, quash, annul, nullify, disqualify, put/make an end to, make void, reject, prohibit

band *n.* 1. group, gang, company, troop, pack, flock, herd
2. strip, stripe, border, bar, collar, ribbon

bandit *n.* brigand, robber, outlaw, criminal, crook, gangster, ruffian, highwayman, mugger

bang *n.* 1. loud noise/sound, burst, explosion, report, crash
2. bump, thump, blow, knock, thud

banish *v.* exile, send away, remove from, oust, cast out, outlaw

bar *v.* forbid, ban, not permit/allow, disallow, disqualify, reject
n. 1. beam, girder, rod, pole, barrier, counter, barricade
2. strip, stripe, line, band

bare *a.* naked, bald, uncovered, unclothed, unfurnished, undisguised, unadorned, empty, scanty, meager

barely *adv.* merely, only just, scarcely, almost, nearly, not quite

barren *a.* fruitless, infertile, empty, dull, unprofitable, worthless

barrier *n.* bar, barricade, gate, fence, hedge, obstacle, blockade, obstruction, hindrance

base *n.* bottom, foot, foundation, pedestal, support
a. low, vulgar, despicable, despised, contemptible, mean, selfish, cowardly, immoral, worthless, ignoble, corrupt, depraved, vile

bashful *a.* shy, easily embarrassed, shamefaced, sheepish

basis *n.* 1. principle, foundation, grounds
2. main/chief part/ portion/ingredient

battle *n.* conflict, encounter, fray, fight, struggle, combat, strife, skirmish, action

beam *n.* 1. bar, girder, crosspiece, plank, lever, rod
2. ray/shaft of light/ electromagnetic waves

bear *v.* 1. carry, support, hold, uphold, transport, yield, produce
2. suffer, endure, abide, put up with, stand, tolerate
bear out: *confirm, substantiate, warrant, guarantee*

beast *n.* animal, brute, creature, quadruped, savage

beautiful *a.* fair, lovely, pretty, handsome, good-looking, beauteous, attractive, delightful, charming, splendid, fine, enchanting

become *v.* 1. change to/into, commence/begin to be
2. suit, befit, adorn

becoming *a.* suitable, fitting, befitting, appropriate

before *adv.* in front/advance, ahead, earlier, beforehand, already, preceding

befriend *v.* be a friend to, be friendly with, accept as a friend, aid, assist, help, favor

beg *v.* ask for, request, implore, plead, entreat, beseech, pray, appeal to, exhort

beggarly *a.* 1. very small, little, slight, trifling, mean, meager, inadequate
2. poor, shabby, sordid, vagrant

begin *v.* commence, start, take the first step, go/set to work

behave *v.* act, act properly/ correctly/with propriety/ with courtesy/with discretion/mannerly

behind *adv.* behindhand, in arrears, in/to the rear, backward, at/to the back/rear, back, after, afterwards, late, belated, retarded

belief *n.* knowledge, faith, trust, confidence, thought, opinion, intuition

belly *n.* abdomen, bowels, intestines
belly-ache: *stomach-ache, abdominal pains, colic*

belong *v.* be attached/situated/sited, be part/the business/the concern/the property of, apply, pertain, appertain, be associated with

belongings *n.* personal property, baggage, luggage

below *adv.* under, underneath, beneath, at/to a lower level, downstairs, downstream, in hell
prep. at/to a greater depth than, lower/lesser than (in size, position, rank or degree)

bend *v.* turn, curve, twist, make/become angular, incline

beneath *prep.* inferior to, not worthy of

benefit *n.* advantage, gain, profit, help, aid, assistance, favor, allowance, pension, privilege, "perk"

benevolent *a.* kindly, helpful, magnanimous, big-hearted, generous, bountiful, munificent, charitable, well-disposed, ready to help, philanthropic

beside *prep.* close to, near, by, on/at a level with, alongside, adjacent to

best *a.* of the most excellent kind, in the most excellent way, finest, most suitable/appropriate/fitting

bestial *a.* beast-like, brutish, brutal, cruel, bloodthirsty, wild, savage, barbarous, obscene

bet *v.* put/place a bet on, back, stake, wager, gamble

better *a.* improved, amended, superior, preferable, more desirable
v. improve, amend, surpass

betterment *n.* improvement, advancement, welfare

bewilder *v.* mystify, baffle, puzzle, perplex, confuse

beyond *prep.* out of reach of, on/at the farther side of, past, outside
adv. at a distance, yonder, past, outside
n. the unknown, future life, most distant/remote part of the earth

bicker *v.* quarrel, differ, dispute, argue, wrangle

bid *v.* 1. offer, invite, proclaim, announce
2. greet, salute, acknowledge
I **bid** you goodnight.
3. order, command, instruct

big *a.* large, great, grand, huge, giant, gigantic, vast, immense, tremendous, enormous, enlarged, swollen, impressive, important, serious, momentous

bill *n.* 1. invoice, account, statement of account
2. notice, poster, placard, program, menu
handbill: *printed notice, leaflet*

bind *v.* join, unite, fasten, hold/tie together, marry

bit *n.* small piece/part/portion/fraction, fragment, morsel, chip, splinter

bite *v.* nip, sting, wound (with teeth), grip

bitter *a.* not sweet, biting, harsh, unrelenting, relentless, virulent, extremely/piercingly cold, resentful, disappointed

blame *v.* accuse, find fault with, charge, lay fault/trouble on, put responsibility on

blank *a.* empty, vacant, not written/printed on

blatant *a.* noisy, loud-voiced, clamorous, flagrant, palpable, undisguised, open, obvious

blaze *n.* bright flame/fire/light/illumination

bleak *a.* dreary, drab, dull, uninteresting, bare, exposed, windswept, chilly, austere

blemish *n.* defect, error, flaw, stain, bad quality, injury
v. taint, mar, sully, spoil the beauty/quality of

blend *v.* mix, mingle, become one, unite, merge, match, harmonize

blessed *a.* holy, consecrated, sacred, sacrosanct, revered, fortunate, lucky, well-favored, blissful

blind *a.* 1. without sight, sightless, unseeing
2. unknowing, not aware, unaware, without discernment/foresight/understanding/appreciation

block *v.* stop, obstruct, wedge, fill up, oppose, hinder

bloodthirsty *a.* desirous of/eager for/wanting bloodshed, cruel, brutal, bestial, wild, savage, barbarous

blossom *n.* bloom, flower, inflorescence

blot *n.* spot, stain, mark, dark patch, blemish, disfigurement

blow *n.* 1. knock, hit, stroke, bang, jab, buffet, cuff, punch, rap, tap
2. shock, mishap, misfortune, bad/ill luck, disaster, calamity, loss, bad news
3. puff, pant, gasp, gust

bluff *a.* abrupt, outspoken, frank, candid, blunt, sincere, genial, cordial, vigorous, abundant
n. deception, pretense, idle/empty threat

blunder *v.* 1. make/commit a mistake/error/indiscretion, mismanage/mishandle a situation
2. move/walk clumsily/blindly, act/behave awkwardly, stumble, trip, fall over
n. mistake, error, oversight, indiscretion, foolish/stupid/silly/compromising/embarrassing act/conduct, *faux pas*

blurred *a.* indistinct, obscure, dim, not clear, hazy, misty, nebulous, confused, sullied, disfigured, smeared, stained, blemished, marked

boast *n.* brag, vanity, vainglory, pride, bombast, swagger, pretension
v. brag, vaunt, exaggerate, swank

body *n.* 1. trunk, torso, physique, figure, frame, form, anatomy
2. corpse, cadaver, remains
3. mass, amount, quantity, group, company, crowd, association, organization, corporation

bog *n.* marsh, morass, mire, quagmire, swamp, slough, fen

bogus *a.* false, fictitious, sham, forged, counterfeit

bold *a.* forward, saucy, cheeky, pert, impertinent, impudent, audacious, brave, daring, reckless, not afraid, fearless, courageous, determined, resolute

bond *n.* 1. joint, union, knot, tie, link, marriage
2. agreement, contract, promise to pay

bondage *n.* slavery, serfdom, servitude, imprisonment, confinement, restraint, subjection

bonus *n.* goodwill payment, extra payment/dividend/ distribution, gratuity, something beneficial/to the good/into the bargain

booty *n.* plunder, loot, profit, gain, reward, prize, treasure

border *n.* edge, margin, division, dividing/demarcation line, boundary, frontier

bore *v.* 1. drill, pierce, make a hole
2. be tiresome/wearisome, uninteresting/a nuisance
n. hole, diameter (of a hole), caliber (of a gun)

borrow *v.* take/obtain a loan, adopt, derive

bottle *n.* flask, carafe, flagon, jar, vial, phial, vessel

bough *n.* branch, arm

bound *n.* 1. leap, jump, spring, gambol
2. limit, boundary

boundless *a.* without limit, unlimited, limitless, endless, infinite

bout *n.* 1. spell/turn of work/ exercise, attack/fit of illness/drinking, spasm, sudden occurrence
2. trial of strength, contest, battle, fight, conflict

bowels *n.* intestines, belly, abdomen, lower part of body

boycott *v.* shun, ignore, avoid, disregard, eschew, cold-shoulder

branch *n.* bough, arm, limb, tributary, outgrowth, projection, line, subdivision

brat *n.* urchin, naughty/ mischievous/roguish child

bravado *n.* defiance, show/display of bravery/courage, pretended bravery/boldness

brave *a.* courageous, bold, daring, dashing, fearless, plucky, valiant, valorous, dauntless, undaunted, heroic, gallant

brawl *v.* quarrel, squabble, fight

brawny *a.* muscular, strong, powerful, vigorous

break *v.* fracture, crack, shatter, splinter, sever, split, damage
break down: *fall, collapse, demolish, decompose, analyze*
break in/into: *enter, breach*
break up: *dismiss, disintegrate, decay, decompose*

brief *a.* short, concise, not long, succinct, terse, summarized, laconic

bright *a.* 1. shining, gleaming, brilliant, radiant, lustrous, glowing, lit up, glossy
2. clever, smart, intelligent, quick-witted, alert, talented, vivacious

brilliant *a.* 1. bright, shining, gleaming, lustrous, sparkling, twinkling, scintillating
2. very clever/intelligent/ talented/gifted, illustrious

bring *v.* carry to/from, bear, convey, transport, fetch, lead, guide
bring about/to pass: *cause to happen/occur*
bring down: *abase, ruin, wound, kill, destroy*
bring to mind: *recall, recollect, remember*

brink *n.* edge, border, brim

brisk *a.* quick, quick-moving, rapid, fast, lively, energetic, vigorous, keen, enlivening, stimulating

brittle *a.* fragile, breakable, apt/liable to break, easily broken/fractured, frail, delicate, weak

broad *a.* wide, not narrow, extensive, expansive, comprehensive, all-embracing, complete, open, full, clear, explicit, main, large

broadcast *v.* distribute, scatter, sow, disseminate, transmit, announce, advertise
n. radio/television transmission

browse *v.* 1. graze, nibble
2. read fitfully/without concentration

brutal *a.* bestial, beastly, cruel, savage, wild, barbarous, depraved, obscene

build *v.* put up, put/fit together, assemble, erect, construct, make, manufacture, fabricate, fashion, establish, institute, develop

bulk *n.* size, amount, quantity, capacity, volume, mass, main part/portion/fraction, contents

bully *v.* browbeat, bluster, threaten, badger, bother, pester, persecute, oppress, hector

bump *n.* 1. noise, sound, bang, thud
2. thump, blow, rap, hit, stroke, jolt

bumptious *a.* conceited, vain, self-opinionated, self-centered, proud, egotistical, boastful, bombastic

bunch *n.* cluster, small group, knot, handful

burden *n.* 1. load, weight, capacity
2. worry, problem, anxiety, responsibility

burn *v.* set on fire, blaze, flame, ignite, incinerate, consume (by fire), cremate

burst *v.* fly/split apart/open, explode, collapse, disintegrate

business *n.* 1. matter, affair, agenda
2. task, job, work, trade, commerce, employment, occupation, profession, vocation

busy *a.* active, fully occupied, working, employed, engaged, diligent
busybody: *fussy/interfering/meddlesome person*

butcher *v.* kill, slaughter, slay, murder, massacre

buy *v.* purchase

bystander *n.* onlooker, spectator, eyewitness, witness

C c

café *n.* coffee-shop, tea-shop, restaurant

calculate *v.* work out, estimate, determine, assess, reckon, compute

call *v.* 1. shout, cry, hail, greet
2. name, address as, know as
3. summon, invite, send for
4. proclaim, announce, signal
call on: *visit*

calm *a.* gentle, peaceful, quiet, easy, relaxed, composed, serene, placid, unruffled, matter of fact, undisturbed, still, windless

camouflage *v.* disguise, hide, conceal, cover, mask

cancel *v.* cross out, delete, erase, remove, withdraw

capable *a.* able, efficient, skillful, proficient, competent, clever, talented, qualified

capital *a.* 1. chief, main, principal, largest, leading
2. fine, excellent, splendid, superb
n. 1. main/chief city
2. assets, wealth

capsize *v.* overturn, tip over, upset

captain *n.* company-commander (army), leader, chief, head, commander of ship/aircraft, master, skipper

capture *a.* catch, seize, arrest, trap, snare, ensnare, grasp, grab, take, get

car *n.* motorcar, automobile, vehicle, carriage

care *n.* 1. attention, interest, regard, consideration, trouble, pains
2. concern, worry, anxiety
3. caution, watchfulness, prudence, vigilance, wariness

career *n.* profession, vocation, calling, development, progress
v. run/go swiftly/wildly

careless *a.* uncaring, thoughtless, heedless, not careful/ cautious/prudent, imprudent; incautious, unmindful

cargo *n.* goods, freight, load, shipment

carry *v.* fetch, convey, transport, transfer

case *v.* enclose, cover, contain
n. 1. container, box, holder, crate
2. event, occurrence, matter, business, example, instance
3. lawsuit, action

cash *n.* money, coins, currency, funds

cast *v.* 1. throw, pitch, toss, heave, fling
2. drop, shed, let fall
3. mould, shape, form
n. actors, performers

casual *a.* easygoing, not arranged, informal, incautious, uncaring, negligent, careless

catch *v.* grasp, hold, seize, get, grip, capture, take, arrest, trap, snare, ensnare
catch up with: *draw level with*

cause *n.* reason, purpose, start, beginning, origin
v. make happen/occur, force, compel

cautious *a.* careful, heedful, mindful, watchful, vigilant, prudent, wary

cease *v.* stop, end, finish, conclude, terminate

ceaseless *a.* without ceasing/ending, unceasing, incessant, never-ending, constant

celebrate *v.* make merry, be festive, rejoice, observe, keep, honor, praise, laud, applaud

center *n.* middle, midpoint, midst, core, heart, kernel

ceremony *n.* solemn/stately/formal celebration/occasion/function/custom/performance, rite

certain *a.* 1. sure, definite, without doubt
2. particular, specific

challenge *n.* dare, defy, question, oppose, contend

champion *n.* 1. victor, winner
2. defender, supporter, protector
a. unbeaten, unequalled, unsurpassed, best, supreme

chance *n.* 1. risk, gamble
2. luck, fortune, fate, accident

change *v.* alter, substitute, adjust, vary, modify, convert, transform

chaos *n.* disorder, confusion, panic, turmoil, tumult

character *n.* 1. nature, quality, type, sort, caliber, disposition
2. reputation
3. person (in a story, play or film)

charge *n.* 1. attack, onslaught, stampede, rush
2. accusation, indictment
3. price, cost, amount, expense
in charge: *responsible*

charm *v.* 1. please, delight, attract, entice, captivate
2. bewitch, enchant, entrance
n. good luck/lucky token/trinket, magic, spell

chart *n.* map, plan, diagram

chat *v.* talk, converse, gossip, chatter

cheap *a.* inexpensive, not dear/costly, of little value, low-priced

cheat *v.* deceive, trick, dupe, swindle, defraud
n. swindler, trickster, fraud

check *v.* 1. slow down, hinder, impede, retard, stop, arrest, halt
2. test, examine, inspect, investigate
3. rebuke, reprove

cheek *n.* audacity, impudence, impertinence, sauce

cheer *v.* 1. please, gladden, hearten, encourage
2. applaud, shout for

chest *n.* 1. breast, bosom, thorax
2. box, case, crate

chew *v.* masticate, grind, crunch, gnaw

chief *a.* main, principal, head, most important, largest, leading
n. chieftain, head, director, leader, captain

child *n.* infant, baby, minor

chill *v.* cool, make cold, refrigerate
a. frigid, cold, chilly, unemotional, unfeeling
n. feverish shivering, cold

chip *n.* tiny piece/part/chunk, splinter, fragment

choke *v.* smother, strangle, asphyxiate

choose *v.* opt, pick, prefer, favor, select, elect

chop *v.* cut, hack, incise, chip, slash, hew

chore *n.* task, job, menial duty

chum *n.* friend, companion, mate, comrade

civil *a.* courteous, polite, well-mannered, gracious

claim *v.* demand, ask for

clamp *v.* clasp, grip, brace

clash *v.* 1. collide
2. contrast, produce disharmony, differ
3. disagree, dispute, quarrel

clasp *v.* clamp, grip, embrace, grasp, buckle, clutch, grab, snatch, hold

class *n.* group, set, category, grade, kind, sort, type, arrangement, selection

clean *v.* free from/remove dirt, wash, tidy, disinfect
a. not dirty, unsoiled, pure

clear *a.* 1. plain, distinct, bright, cloudless, transparent, apparent, obvious
2. open, without hindrance/obstacles

clever *a.* intelligent, talented, skillful, ingenious, smart, bright, wise, shrewd, resourceful, adroit

climb *v.* ascend, mount, go/come up, scale

cling *v.* hold, clasp, clutch, stick, adhere

cloak *n.* 1. coat, mantle, shawl, wrap
2. pretense, cover, concealment, disguise, mask

close *v.* 1. shut, seal, cover
2. end, conclude, finish, terminate, complete

cloth *n.* fabric, material, textile

clothe *v.* dress, attire, garb, cover

clothing *n.* clothes, garments, attire, apparel, garb, dress, costume

clown *n.* jester, fool, buffoon, idiot, joker

club *n.* 1. stick, cudgel, truncheon, bat, baton
2. society, group, circle, association

clue *n.* hint, guide, lead, key, suggestion, indication, inkling

clumsy *a.* awkward, ungainly, bungling, unskilled, not skillful, ungraceful

clutch *v.* hold, embrace, grab, seize, snatch, clasp, clamp, grip, grasp

coach *n.* 1. carriage, car
2. teacher, instructor, tutor, trainer
v. teach, train, instruct

coarse *a.* 1. not smooth, rough, matte, harsh, jagged
2. vulgar, common, uncouth, boorish, loutish, ill-mannered

coat *n.* jacket, garment, cover, covering, film, layer, fur, hair, wool

coax *v.* encourage, persuade, entice, tempt, wheedle, cajole

code *n.* 1. system, pattern
2. secret signs/signals/words
3. set of rules/regulations/laws

coil *n.* spiral, helix
v. wind, turn, encircle, wrap around

cold *a.* 1. chilly, cool, icy, freezing, frozen, frigid, wintry
2. distant, unfeeling, unemotional, cold-blooded
3. chill, feverish, shivering

collapse *v.* break down, fall, fall down, give way, cave in

collect *v.* gather, pick, store, assemble, bring together

collide *v.* meet, hit, crash, smash

color *n.* dye, paint, pigment, shade, hue, tint, stain

colossal *a.* gigantic, huge, massive, enormous, immense, tremendous, vast

combat *n.* fight, battle, encounter, struggle, action, fray, contest, engagement

combine *v.* join, unite, cooperate, blend, merge, mix

come *v.* arrive, advance, draw near, happen, occur

comfort *n.* ease, luxury, contentment
v. console, sympathize with, cheer up, hearten, soothe

comic *a.* comical, funny, amusing, laughable, humorous, facetious, droll

command *v.* control, direct, take charge of, order, bid, instruct, require, rule, regulate, dictate

commence *v.* begin, start, initiate, instigate

commit *v.* 1. do, perform, act
2. entrust, consign, send, deliver

common *a.* ordinary, commonplace, plain, vulgar, normal, standard, usual, everyday, average, cheap, widespread, well-known, customary, public

companion *n.* friend, comrade, chum, pal, mate

company *n.* 1. group, assembly, gathering, band, gang, crew, troop, party, contingent
2. firm, business, syndicate
3. friends, companions, visitors

compare *v.* liken, be similar/alike, match, balance, harmonize

compel *v.* force, make, drive, press

compete *v.* strive, vie, participate, contest, struggle

competent *a.* able, capable, efficient, skilled, qualified, fit, suited

complain *v.* grumble, express discontent/dissatisfaction/displeasure, protest, nag

complete *v.* finish, end, conclude, close, terminate
a. whole, full, total, entire, comprehensive, perfect, absolute

compliment *v.* praise, congratulate

compose *v.* 1. put together, compile, form, create, invent, originate
2. calm, contain, restrain

conceal *v.* hide, cover, disguise, mask, camouflage, keep secret

conceit *n.* pride, vanity, pomposity

concentrate *v.* think carefully, pay attention/regard

concern *n.* 1. worry, anxiety, bother, upset, distress, interest
2. affair, business, matter, project, enterprise, scheme, plan, venture

concerning *prep.* about, of, to do/concerned with

conclude *v.* 1. end, finish, terminate, complete, close
2. decide, gather, reason, assume

condemn	*v.*	blame, accuse, denounce, convict
condense	*v.*	reduce, contract, shorten, summarize, compress
condition	*n.*	1. state, nature, quality, grade, tone, texture, age 2. provision, stipulation, proviso
conduct	*v.*	1. lead, guide, escort, direct, manage, control 2. carry, convey, transport, transmit
conduct	*n.*	behavior, bearing, carriage
confess	*v.*	admit, own up, declare, acknowledge
confident	*a.*	certain, sure, secure, hopeful, optimistic
confidential	*a.*	not to be disclosed/revealed/repeated, secret
confine	*v.*	keep in, enclose, contain, cage, imprison, incarcerate
confuse	*v.*	1. mix up, disorder, disarrange, disturb, disarray, jumble, make/cause chaos 2. bewilder, mystify, puzzle, confound, perplex
connect	*v.*	join, unite, fasten, attach, combine, bind, tie, link, couple
conquer	*v.*	beat, defeat, vanquish, overcome, overpower, crush, subdue
consider	*v.*	think about, reflect on, ponder on, heed, pay attention/regard to
considerable	*a.*	large, great, ample, abundant, copious, generous, plentiful
considerate	*a.*	thoughtful, mindful, kind, unselfish, benevolent
construct	*v.*	build, make, erect, put up/together, assemble, compile, compose
consume	*v.*	1. use up, spend, waste/burn away, corrode, rust 2. eat, devour, swallow, drink, imbibe
contain	*v.*	1. hold, comprise, enclose, include 2. calm, restrain, compose
content	*a.*	happy, pleased, glad, satisfied
content	*n.*	filling, constituents, ingredients, capacity, volume
contest	*v.*	dispute, try to disprove, invalidate, argue
contest	*n.*	struggle, combat, battle, competition, dispute, feud, encounter
continue	*v.*	carry/go on, proceed, prolong, extend, add to, keep up
contract	*v.*	1. shorten, condense, reduce, summarize, shrink 2. agree, promise, undertake
contradict	*v.*	deny, gainsay, rebut, refute
control	*v.*	direct, command, regulate, lead, guide, manage, drive
convenient	*a.*	fit, suitable, handy, at hand, available
conversation	*n.*	talk, chat, discussion
cool	*a.*	1. cold, chilly 2. calm, quiet, tranquil, restrained, deliberate, distant
copy	*v.*	imitate, reproduce, duplicate, rewrite, mock, mimic
core	*n.*	center, middle, heart, kernel
correct	*a.*	right, proper, just, exact, accurate
correspond	*v.*	1. agree, match, fit 2. write/send letters, communicate
cost	*n.*	price, value, charge, expense

costly *a.* expensive, dear, highly-priced, valuable

costume *n.* dress, attire, garb, apparel, uniform, suit, robe, outfit

council *n.* assembly, meeting, gathering, convention

count *v.* 1. number, reckon, score, calculate, compute
2. matter, signify, be significant/important
3. depend, rely, plan

couple *n.* pair, two, twosome, duet
v. join, link, tie, connect, unite, bind

courage *n.* bravery, valor, heroism, boldness, fearlessness, pluck

course *n.* 1. route, way, road, path, direction, current
2. method, technique, plan, progress
v. hunt, chase, pursue

courtesy *n.* politeness, good manners, etiquette, civility, respect

cover *v.* conceal, hide, cloak, shield, screen, shelter, enclose, include

crack *v.* split, fracture, break, splinter

crafty *a.* sly, cunning, artful, devious, deceitful, shrewd

cram *v.* overfill, stuff, jam, ram

crash *n.* 1. loud noise, bang, smash
2. collision, impact
3. failure, ruin

crawl *v.* creep, clamber

crazy *a.* foolish, silly, absurd, mad, nonsensical, irrational

create *v.* make, devise, design, originate, invent, produce

creature *n.* 1. animal, beast
2. wretch, unfortunate/miserable/despicable person

credit *n.* reputation, honor, integrity
v. believe, accept, acknowledge

crew *n.* gang, group, team, band, company

crime *n.* wrongdoing, offense, sin, misdeed, felony

crisp *a.* brittle, crusty, snappy

criticize *v.* find fault, judge, complain

crop *n.* 1. harvest, produce, yield
2. riding-whip
v. trim, cut short, reap

cross *v.* 1. travel across, traverse
2. oppose, defy
a. angry, annoyed, upset

crowd *n.* gathering, group, mass, throng, assembly, mob, multitude

crude *a.* 1. raw, rough, unrefined, natural, native, unpolished
2. uncouth, coarse, vulgar, ill-mannered, ungracious

cruel *a.* hurtful, spiteful, unkind, inhuman, inhumane, vindictive, vicious, brutal, savage, barbarous

cruise *v.* sail, voyage

crumble *v.* fall/break into pieces, disintegrate

crush *v.* 1. crunch, grind, press, squeeze, squash, trample
2. overcome, overpower, subdue, quell, defeat, beat

crust *n.* rind, shell, outer layer, covering

cry *v.* 1. shout, yell, call out, scream
2. weep, sob, bawl, whine, whimper

culprit *n.* offender, guilty person

cultivate *v.* farm, grow crops, plow, dig, till, improve

cunning *a.* sly, crafty, artful, devious, deceitful, shrewd, clever, skillful, ingenious

curb *v.* check, control, curtail, bridle, restrict, limit, restrain, hold/keep back

cure *v.* heal, make well, relieve, restore, remedy, put right, correct, repair

curious *a.* 1. inquisitive, prying, searching, inquiring
2. interesting, strange, odd, unusual, peculiar, queer

current *n.* flow, stream, course
a. prevailing, present, common, popular, accepted, widespread

curse *v.* 1. swear, blaspheme
2. wish/bring evil upon, condemn, damn
n. suffering, bane

curve *n.* bend, turn, curvature, arch, arc

custom *n.* habit, rule, fashion, practice, manner, tradition

customer *n.* buyer, purchaser, client

cut *v.* 1. divide, sever, wound, gash, slash, slit, puncture, clip, snip
2. ignore, cold-shoulder, boycott

D d

dabble *v.* 1. wet, moisten, splash
2. have a go, try out, meddle, participate, take part

daily *adv.* every day, each day, often, frequently
n. newspaper, journal

dainty *a.* 1. neat, nice, delicate, pleasing, choice, tasteful, refined, exquisite
2. clean, particular, fastidious

damage *v.* injure, hurt, harm, afflict, disfigure, break, abuse, sabotage

damp *v.* 1. dampen, moisten, make humid
2. discourage
Her indifference **damped** his ardor.

danger *n.* risk, peril, threat, menace, hazard, jeopardy

dare *v.* 1. attempt, venture
2. challenge, defy

daring *a.* bold, brave, valiant, venturesome, adventurous, fearless, courageous, undaunted

dark *a.* without light/illumination, unlit, sunless, dim, dull, somber, gloomy, murky, indistinct, obscure, drab, dreary, cheerless

darling *n.* sweetheart, dearest, pet, favorite, loved one, beloved

dart *v.* fly, spring, run, rush, dash, race, spurt
n. arrow, missile, javelin

dash *v.* 1. run quickly/swiftly/speedily/fast/rapidly, race, sprint, spurt
2. smash/crash/bang on/against
3. discourage, spoil, frustrate

dawn *n.* 1. daybreak, break of day, sunrise
2. beginning, start, commencement, origin
dawn on: *grow/become clear/plain to*

day *n.* 1. daylight, daytime
2. 24 hours

daydream *v.* fancy, imagine, build castles in the air, have pipe-dreams, fantasize

daze *v.* bewilder, confuse, mix up, stun

dazzle *v.* blind, confuse
n. glare, blinding light

dead *a.* numb, insensitive, dull, lifeless, not living/alive, deceased, extinct

deaden *v.* numb, dull, diminish, soften, lessen, soothe, alleviate, cushion, muffle, smother

deadly *a.* fatal, mortal, lethal, destructive, poisonous, harmful

deaf *a.* 1. unable to hear
2. unwilling to hear/listen, heedless, inattentive, unmindful

deal *v.* 1. handle, manage
2. trade, do business
3. deliver, distribute, give/hand out

dealer *n.* trader, merchant, distributor, wholesaler, shopkeeper, retailer

dear *a.* 1. dearest, darling, beloved, cherished, favorite
2. not cheap, costly, expensive

debate	*v.*	argue, discuss, dispute, contest, wrangle
debt	*n.*	debit, money/property owed/owing, due, duty, obligation
decay	*v.*	rot, wither, fade, waste away, deteriorate, putrefy, decompose, spoil, rust, corrode
deceive	*v.*	cheat, swindle, hoax, mislead, trick, fool, bluff, dissemble
decent	*a.*	proper, respectable, becoming, seemly, modest, not vulgar/rude/obscene
decide	*v.*	settle, fix, arrange, rule, resolve, determine, conclude
declare	*v.*	state, announce, proclaim, admit, reveal, assert
decline	*v.*	1. refuse, reject, not accept 2. drop, lessen, reduce, depreciate, decrease, diminish, fall lower, weaken, become feeble/frail/infirm
decorate	*v.*	beautify, adorn
decrease	*v.*	lessen, reduce, diminish, lower, shrink, contract, drop, fall, decline, depreciate, soften
deed	*n.*	act, action, feat, performance
defeat	*v.*	beat, overcome, overpower, subdue, conquer, vanquish, quell, rout
	n.	failure, loss
defect	*n.*	fault, flaw, blemish, imperfection
	v.	desert, run away
defend	*v.*	protect, maintain, guard, shield, support
definite	*a.*	exact, fixed, accurate, precise, certain, sure, clear, distinct, decided
deformed	*a.*	misshapen, malformed, warped, twisted, distorted, disfigured, crippled, lame
defraud	*v.*	cheat, swindle, rob, deceive, trick
defy	*v.*	1. dare, challenge, resist, oppose, mock 2. disregard, ignore, flout
delay	*v.*	1. postpone, put back, retard, hinder 2. linger, loiter, dawdle, hang about, hesitate, wait
deliberate	*a.*	intentional, fully considered
deliberate	*v.*	consider, think over/about
delicacy	*n.*	1. weakness, feebleness, tenderness, daintiness, fineness, diplomacy 2. fine/dainty/tasty food
delicate	*a.*	1. fine, dainty, tender, fragile 2. feeble, weak, frail, infirm
delicious	*a.*	tasty, sweet, luscious, dainty, enjoyable, pleasing
delight	*v.*	please, charm, thrill, make happy/glad/joyful, enchant, entrance, amuse, entertain
deliver	*v.*	1. hand over, transfer, bring, distribute 2. set free, liberate, rescue, save
demand	*v.*	ask, claim, request, apply, urge
demolish	*v.*	destroy, put down, wreck, ruin, smash, raze
den	*n.*	nest, lair, retreat, cave
dense	*a.*	1. thick, concentrated, compact, solid, close, lush 2. stupid, slow-minded
deny	*v.*	1. contradict, gainsay, dispute, disprove, refute 2. refuse, withhold

depart *v.* leave, go, go away, go/start out, withdraw, quit

depend *v.* rely, trust/be confident in

depression *n.* 1. hollow, dent, cavity, indentation
2. sadness, misery, unhappiness, gloominess, dejection

deputy *n.* substitute, assistant, agent, representative, delegate

derelict *a.* forsaken, abandoned, vacated, deserted, neglected

descend *v.* go/get down, drop, fall, sink, settle, dismount, alight

descent *n.* fall, drop, slope, incline, declivity

describe *v.* write/speak/talk about, explain, report on, outline, express

desert *v.* forsake, abandon, leave, vacate, neglect

desert *a.* barren, empty, infertile
n. barren/empty/infertile land

deserted *a.* empty, vacant, forsaken, abandoned

deserve *v.* earn, merit, win, rate, be worthy of

design *n.* 1. pattern, decoration, plan, sketch, drawing
2. intention, object, aim, scheme, idea, notion, creation

desirable *a.* wanted, desired, worthy, worthwhile, acceptable, good

desire *v.* want, wish/crave/yearn for

desolate *a.* 1. lone, alone, forlorn, unhappy, sad, wretched, miserable
2. lonely, deserted

despair *n.* discouragement, hopelessness, pessimism

desperate *a.* 1. rash, reckless, bold, wild, savage, ferocious, careless
2. hopeless, unpromising

despise *v.* scorn, treat with contempt, dislike, disapprove of

destroy *v.* pull/knock down, demolish, end, finish, wreck, ruin, smash, raze, annihilate

detach *v.* take/pull off, remove, disconnect, loosen, unfasten, separate

detain *v.* hold, arrest, keep waiting, retard, delay, hinder

detect *v.* find, discover, notice, see, perceive, observe

detective *n.* investigator, sleuth

determine *v.* decide, resolve, arrange, assess, estimate, find out, learn

determined *a.* firm, adamant, resolved, resolute, stubborn, obdurate, obstinate

detest *v.* hate, dislike intensely, abhor, loathe

develop *v.* improve slowly/gradually, expand, enlarge, increase, extend

device *n.* 1. gadget, contrivance, invention, apparatus, trick, scheme, plan, arrangement

devoted *a.* loyal, faithful, true, constant, dedicated, earnest, sincere

devour *v.* consume, eat up greedily/voraciously, swallow

dictate *v.* 1. give orders/instructions/commands/directions
2. say, tell

die *v.* expire, depart, fade/pass away, wither, decline, perish

different *a.* dissimilar, unusual, uncommon, special, novel, unalike, not alike

difficulty *n.* problem, snag, obstacle, dilemma, complication, bother, trouble, burden, hardship, plight, predicament

dignity *n.* eminence, worthiness, pride, grandeur, majesty, nobility, stateliness

diligent *a.* industrious, hard-working, constant, steady, assiduous

dim *a.* dull, faint, indistinct, obscure, vague, dark, cloudy, inconspicuous

din *n.* row, noise, uproar, babble, clamor, tumult, racket, bedlam, pandemonium

dingy *a.* shabby, faded, grimy, dirty, squalid

dip *n.*
1. immersion, dive
2. swim, bathe
3. hollow, downwards slope

direct *a.*
1. straight, express, short
2. outspoken

v.
1. govern, control, order, command, manage
2. address, send, aim, conduct

direction *n.*
1. way, course, aim, route, path
2. order, instruction, rule, regulation

directly *adv.* at once, immediately, now

dirt *n.* muck, mud, soil, soot, filth, impurity, pollution, contamination, squalor

disaster *n.* catastrophe, tragedy, calamity, great misfortune

discipline *n.* obedience, order, instruction, training, control, self-control

discuss *v.* debate, talk over

disgrace *v.* put to shame, dishonor, disfavor, defame, degrade

disguise *v.* hide, conceal, mask, camouflage, veil

disgusting *a.* revolting, repulsive, loathsome, nasty, disgraceful

dismal *a.* dreary, drab, not cheerful, cheerless, dingy, sad, miserable, doleful, gloomy, mournful, lugubrious

dismiss *v.* send away/off, discharge

displace *v.* take/change the place of, remove, move, shift, disarrange

display *n.* show, exhibition, parade, presentation, demonstration

v. show, exhibit, parade, demonstrate

displease *v.* offend, annoy, vex, make indignant

distant *a.*
1. far away/off, remote, at a distance
2. cold, frigid, indifferent, shy, reticent, reserved

distinct *a.*
1. clear, plain, definite, obvious
2. separate, different, unconnected

distress *n.* trouble, grief, worry, concern, anxiety, unhappiness, sadness, misery, discomfort, pain

distribute *v.* hand/give out, deal, share, broadcast, scatter, sow

distrust *n.* doubt, disbelief, suspicion

disturb *v.* bother, worry, pester, molest, agitate, annoy, irritate, upset

divide *v.* separate, cut, break up, part, distribute, share

do *v.* make, act, accomplish, perform, achieve

dodge *v.* avoid, evade, move aside, duck, side-step

n. device, trick, scheme, plan

donate *v.* give, contribute, present

doubtful *a.* uncertain, unsure, suspicious, distrustful, dubious, undecided, wavering, indefinite

doubtless *adv.* without a/any doubt, certainly, surely, decidedly, definitely

drab *a.* dull, dreary, shabby, monotonous, tedious, gloomy, plain

drag *v.* pull, haul, tow, tug, draw

drain *v.* empty, flow
n. waste-pipe, gutter, outlet, trench, conduit, channel

drastic *a.* violent, vigorous, ruthless

draw *v.* 1. attract, pull, haul, drag, tow, tug
2. sketch, design

dreadful *a.* fearful, alarming, terrible, awful, horrible, atrocious, dire

dream *n.* fancy, vision, trance, nightmare

dreary *a.* drab, dull, tedious, bleak, barren, cheerless, dismal, dingy, gloomy

dress *n.* clothes, clothing, garments, attire, apparel, garb, costume, robes

drift *v.* wander, float

drill *v.* 1. exercise
2. bore

drive *v.* 1. guide, control, direct, steer, pilot
2. urge, press, persuade, compel, make, prod

drop *n.* 1. fall, descent, dive
2. tiny amount/quantity, ball, globule
3. sip, taste

drown *v.* 1. flood, drench, soak
2. stifle, suffocate, extinguish, muffle, deaden

drowsy *a.* sleepy, sluggish, lethargic, languid

dry *a.* 1. without water/moisture, waterless, arid
2. thirsty, parched
3. dull, boring, tedious, uninteresting, dreary

dual *a.* twofold, double

due *a.* 1. owing, unpaid, payable
2. expected, awaited
3. rightful, suitable, appropriate

dull *a.* 1. dim, not bright, faint, obscure, indistinct, cloudy, sunless
2. blunt
3. stupid, dense, backward

duplicate *v.* copy, imitate, repeat, reproduce

duty *n.* 1. obligation, service, office, function, engagement
2. tax, payment, demand

dwell *v.* live, reside, abide, lodge, inhabit

dwindle *v.* lessen, reduce, diminish, decrease, shrink, fade away

dye *n.* paint, pigment, coloring matter, stain

E e

each *a.* every
pron. each/everyone

eager *a.* keen, enthusiastic, earnest, zealous, greatly desirous, willing, determined, passionate, ardent, fervent

early *adv.* beforehand, before time, in advance
a. long ago, of bygone days/times/ages, former

earn *v.* gain, obtain, acquire, get, achieve, attain, work for, be rewarded with, deserve, merit, rate

earnest *a.* determined, serious, keen, zealous, willing, enthusiastic, passionate, ardent, eager, sincere, honest, true

ease *n.* rest, relaxation, calm, comfort, leisure, quiet, easiness, simplicity
v. reduce, lessen, minimize, relieve, soothe, alleviate, palliate

easy *a.* restful, relaxed, calm, comfortable, leisurely, without effort, effortless not hard/difficult, simple, facile, fluent

eat *v.* 1. dine, consume, feed/feast on, devour
2. wear away, corrode, rust, erode

eccentric *a.* 1. odd, strange, queer, peculiar, unusual, uncommon, bizarre, irregular, whimsical
2. not concentric/circular

edge *n.* margin, boundary, border, verge, rim, brink
v. 1. sharpen
2. make/furnish a border to/for
3. move slowly/little by little, insinuate

edible *a.* eatable, wholesome, nutritious

educate *v.* teach, instruct, train, tutor, enlighten, inform, guide, lead, bring up (children)

effect *n.* result, outcome, consequence, impression
v. do, complete, put into effect, expedite, accomplish

effective *a.* 1. able, capable, competent, efficient, actual, existing
2. striking, pleasing, attractive

efficient *a.* able, capable, competent, effective, skillful, well-organized, well-managed, business-like

effort *n.* 1. attempt, try, endeavor, essay, application
2. work, labor, toil, industry, exertion, energy, action, activity

elaborate *a.* decorative, ornamental, elegant, ornate, overdone

elaborate *v.* explain, specify, exaggerate, embroider, expand, extend

elapse *v.* go/pass by/away

elastic *a.* springy, stretchy, pliable, flexible, resilient, supple

elated *a.* excited, merry, gleeful, joyful, overjoyed, carried away, overcome

elect *v.* choose, select, pick
n. best, most worthy/deserving, privileged

elegant *a.* graceful, beautiful, handsome, stylish, tasteful, refined, excellent, accomplished

elementary *a.* simple, easy, basic, fundamental, introductory, rudimentary

eliminate *v.* leave out, remove, erase, abolish, expel, discharge

eloquent *a.* well-spoken, fluent, rhetorical

embark *v.* board, go aboard/on board, set out, depart

embarrass *v.* make uncomfortable, discomfort, confuse, disconcert, bewilder, perplex, encumber, impede, complicate

emblem *n.* badge, mark, symbol, sign, token, device, crest

embrace *v.* 1. hug, clasp, cuddle, hold
2. include, contain, comprise, accept eagerly

emerge *v.* come into view, appear, arise

emergency *n.* urgent/desperate situation, crisis, dilemma

eminent *a.* famous, celebrated, renowned, notable, noted, illustrious, exalted

emphasize *v.* stress, accent, accentuate, bring into prominence

employ *v.* use, give work to, find work for, engage, hire, appoint, retain

empty *v.* void, evacuate, pour out, drain, exhaust
a. vacant, unoccupied, deserted, bare, desolate, hollow, bereft

encamp *v.* erect/pitch tents, make/form a camp

enchant *v.* charm, delight, please, captivate, beguile, entrance, bewitch

enclose *v.* contain, surround, encircle, envelop, enfold, wrap, conceal, hide

encounter *v.* meet, come across, bump into

encourage *v.* stimulate, embolden, give support to, inspire, hearten, cheer, invite

end *v.* finish, terminate, cease, stop, conclude, finalize
n. 1. aim, object, intention, result
2. tip, point, extremity

endanger *v.* put/place in danger/jeopardy/peril, imperil

endless *a.* boundless, limitless, everlasting, continual, continuous, ceaseless, incessant, uninterrupted, perpetual, eternal, forever

endure *v.* 1. put up with, bear, suffer, tolerate, submit to, undergo
2. last, exist, live, continue, remain

enemy *n.* foe, adversary, antagonist, opponent

energetic *a.* active, vigorous, lusty, brisk, lively, alive, zestful, enthusiastic, zealous

energy *n.* vigor, power, force, enthusiasm, keenness, zeal, zest, stamina

enfold *v.* enclose, wrap, clasp, embrace, encircle, envelop, surround, conceal, hide, contain

engage *v.* 1. employ, hire, find work for, appoint
2. undertake, promise, guarantee, contract
3. begin to fight/grapple, encounter, attack

engulf *v.* swallow up, envelop, overwhelm

enjoyment *n.* pleasure, delight, joy, happiness, gladness, amusement

enlarge *v.* make larger/bigger/wider, increase, expand, magnify, extend

enlighten *v.* 1. give light to, brighten, illuminate
2. teach, instruct, educate, inform, advise

enormous *a.* giant, gigantic, huge, tremendous, vast, immense, monstrous

enough *a.* ample, adequate, sufficient

enquire *v.* *see* **inquire**

enrage *v.* anger, vex, annoy, make furious, infuriate, madden, aggravate

ensure *v.* make sure/certain/safe

enter *v.* 1. go/come into, invade
2. make an entry, register, record

enterprise *n.* venture, project, plan, scheme, undertaking, task

entertain *v.* amuse, delight, divert, beguile

enthusiasm *n.* keenness, eagerness, zeal, zest, willingness, determination, passion

entice *v.* tempt, lure, attract, bait, coax, persuade, induce

entire *a.* complete, whole, full, total

entrance *n.* entry, way in, opening, approach, access, doorway, gateway

entrance *v.* charm, delight, beguile, captivate, enchant, bewitch

environment *n.* surroundings, habitat, neighborhood

envy *n.* jealousy, desire, covetousness

episode *n.* incident, event, occasion, happening, occurrence

equal *a.* alike, the same, equivalent, identical, even, uniform

equip *v.* supply, provide, furnish, fit out

equivalent *a.* alike, the same, equal

erase *v.* eradicate, rub out, efface, remove

erect *v.* build, construct, assemble, put up, raise
a. upright, perpendicular, vertical

err *v.* make a mistake/error, do wrong, blunder, default, sin

errand *n.* mission, expedition, journey, purpose/object of journey

error *n.* mistake, fault, blunder, wrong

erupt *v.* burst out, explode, blow up, discharge

escape *v.* 1 become free, be free/released/liberated, leak, depart, take flight, flee, make off, steal away
2. avoid, evade, elude, dodge

escort *v.* protect, guard, accompany, guide, lead, conduct

essential *a.* necessary, needful, needed, requisite, vital, fundamental, very important

establish *v.* 1. found, build, institute, set up
2. prove, confirm

estimate *v.* assess, calculate, judge, gauge, measure

eternal *a.* everlasting, for ever, continual, continuous, ceaseless, incessant, perpetual, endless, abiding

evade *v.* avoid, dodge, escape, elude

evaporate *v.* 1. vaporize, become a vapor
2. vanish, disappear, become invisible, dissolve

even *a.* level, flat, smooth, regular, not odd, uniform, exact, exactly divisible by two

event *n.* incident, happening, occurrence, episode, affair, occasion

eventually *adv.* at last, in time, lastly, finally, ultimately

everlasting *a.* eternal, perpetual, for ever, continuous, continual, ceaseless, incessant, endless, abiding

evident *a.* plain, clear, true, obvious, apparent

evil *n.* wickedness, sinfulness, wrongdoing, malevolence, vice, immorality, sin, harm

exact *a.* correct, precise, just, true, definite, accurate
v. demand, insist on

exaggerate *v.* magnify, overstate, romanticize, elaborate, embroider, stretch, enlarge, expand, amplify

examine *v.* check, test, inspect, observe, look at, search, investigate

example *n.* specimen, model, pattern, sample, illustration

exasperate *v.* vex, provoke, irritate, aggravate, annoy

exceed *v.* be more/larger/greater than, surpass, go beyond

excel *v.* be better than/superior to, do well, surpass, beat

excellent *a.* exceptional, outstanding, superior, perfect, superb, admirable

exceptional *a.* outstanding, special, rare, unusual, uncommon, extraordinary

excess *n.* 1. surplus, abundance
2. outrage, intemperance

excite *v.* arouse, enliven, stir, agitate, disturb, stimulate, provoke

exclaim *v.* cry/call out, shout

exclude *v.* leave/shut out, omit, disregard, reject, expel, oust, banish

excursion *n.* trip, outing, journey, expedition, tour

excuse *v.* pardon, overlook, condone, forgive
n. apology, explanation, plea, defense

execute *v.* 1. do, carry out, perform, expedite, effect
2. put to death, kill, liquidate

exercise *n.* task, activity, drill, maneuver

exertion *n.* effort, endeavor, toil, work, labor, industry

exhaust *v.* 1. tire, weary, fatigue, weaken, enfeeble
2. use up, consume, empty, drain

exhibit *v.* display, show, present, reveal, expose

exist *v.* live, survive

exit *n.* way out, outlet, withdrawal, departure

expand *v.* increase, enlarge, magnify, amplify, swell, distend, dilate, extend, stretch, spread

expect *v.* await, anticipate, hope for, look forward to

expel *v.* turn/drive/throw out, eject, banish, exile, oust, send/chase away, exclude

expense *n.* cost, charge, amount, total, sum, outlay

expensive *a.* not cheap, costly, dear, high-priced

experience *v.* undergo, encounter, endure, suffer
n. 1. happening, occurrence, event
2. ordeal, trial
3. practice, training

expert *a.* skillful, adept, proficient, talented, clever, well-qualified, well-trained

explain *v.* clarify, elucidate, elaborate, demonstrate, show

exploit *v.* take advantage of, gain/profit/benefit from, use
n. brave/striking act/action/deed, venture, adventure, escapade, feat, stunt, achievement

explore *v.* search, examine, look at, inspect, survey, reconnoiter

expose *v.* 1. uncover, bare, disclose, show, exhibit
2. discredit

express *a.* quick, fast, rapid, speedy, swift, without delay/interruptions, unretarded
v. state, declare, assert, indicate

expression *n.* 1. statement, remark, declaration, explanation
2. look, show, appearance

exquisite *a.* keen, acute, fine, delicate, dainty, lovely, choice, superb

extend *v.* 1. stretch, elongate, lengthen, expand, enlarge, increase, spread
2. offer, give

extent *n.* size, amount, quantity, expanse, scope

exterior *a.* outside, outer, outward, external

exterminate *v.* destroy, liquidate, abolish, wipe out, kill

external *a.* exterior, outside, outward, outer

extra *a.* additional, supplementary, surplus, spare

extract *n.* quotation, passage (from a book), section, part, portion, essence
v. pull/draw/take out, remove, withdraw

extraordinary *a.* strange, uncommon, unusual, rare, out of the ordinary, incredible, amazing, astounding, remarkable, astonishing

extravagance *n.* reckless/foolish/needless waste, excess, lavishness, liberality

extreme *a.* farthest, utmost, most distant/remote

extremely *adv.* exceedingly, outstandingly, exceptionally

eye *v.* look at, regard, view, observe, watch carefully
eye-opener: *surprise, shock, revelation*

F f

fable *n.* story, tale, legend, myth

fabricate *v.* 1. make, manufacture, construct
2. lie, be untruthful, invent

fabulous *a.* legendary, mythical, fictitious, unreal, fanciful, incredible, astonishing, wonderful, extraordinary

face *n.* 1. visage, countenance
2. front, outside, exterior
v. meet, encounter, confront, oppose, defy

fade *v.* grow/become dim/faint, lose color, wither, droop, wane

fail *v.* 1. miss, neglect, omit, be unsuccessful
2. disappoint, let down
3. weaken, become feeble, decline, deteriorate

faint *v.* swoon, droop, falter, weaken
a. 1. weak, feeble, languid
2. not clear/distinct, unclear, indistinct, dim, vague, faded

fair *a.* 1. just, right, correct, proper, impartial, honest
2. fine, handsome, pleasing, attractive, beautiful
3. bright, clear, fine, sunny
4. average, passable, acceptable
n. market, wake

faith *n.* belief, trust, confidence, devotion, loyalty, religion

faithful *a.* loyal, true, constant, sure, devoted, reliable, dependable, trustworthy, resolute

fake *a.* sham, bogus, fraudulent, counterfeit, forged, false, imitation, not authentic

fall *v.* 1. drop, descend, plunge, tumble, topple, go down
2. lower, lessen, diminish, decline, depreciate

false *a.* 1. sham, imitation, bogus, fake, counterfeit, forged, artificial, fraudulent, not authentic, make-believe, pretentious
2. not true/correct, untrue, incorrect, wrong, mistaken, erroneous
3. disloyal, unfaithful, inconstant, treacherous, not trustworthy

fame *n.* renown, reputation, prestige

familiar *a.* 1. well-known, common, commonplace, ordinary, everyday
2. friendly, informal, sociable, companionable, intimate

family *n.* kith, kin, kindred, folk, tribe, relations, relatives, household

famine *n.* hunger, starvation, dearth/shortage of food

famous *a.* famed, celebrated, great, notable, noted, well-known, illustrious, renowned

fancy *n.* idea, notion, belief, supposition, conjecture, whim, fantasy, imagination
a. decorated, ornamental, ornate, pretty, gaudy

fantastic *a.* fanciful, imagined, whimsical, absurd, weird, strange, peculiar, farfetched, fabulous, wonderful

far *a.* distant, remote
farfetched: *exaggerated, embroidered, romanticized, unbelievable*

fare *v.* 1. live, exist, manage, turn out, be fed/accommodated/entertained
2. go, travel, journey
fare forth: *set/start out*
n. 1. fee, charge, payment (for a journey)
2. food, eatables, victuals, provisions

farewell *n.* good-bye, adieu, leave-taking, parting

farm *v.* cultivate, till
n. farmstead, holding

farther *a.* more distant/remote/extended

fascinate *v.* charm, entrance, enchant, attract, entice

fashion *v.* make, shape, mold, form, design, create, invent
n. style, mode, vogue, custom, tradition, manner, way

fast *a.* 1. quick, rapid, swift, speedy, fleet, lively, nimble, brisk, vigorous
2. secure, stable, fixed, firm, tight
v. hunger, starve, go without food

fasten *v.* secure, fix, attach, tie, knot, bind, join, connect, couple, link, anchor

fat *n.* grease, oil
a. plump, stout, gross, corpulent, obese, well-fed

fatal *a.* deadly, ruinous, mortal, lethal

fate *n.* fortune, luck, lot, destiny, doom

fatigue *v.* tire out, weary, exhaust, enfeeble, weaken

fault *n.* 1. defect, flaw, imperfection, weakness, failing, disadvantage, mistake, error
2. wrong, offense, sin

favor *v.* befriend, be kind to, prefer

favorable *a.* friendly, helpful, kind, kindly, beneficial, useful, promising, hopeful, well-disposed, propitious

fear *n.* dread, terror, fright, horror, dismay, apprehension, alarm

fearless *a.* bold, brave, courageous, gallant, undaunted, dauntless, valiant, daring, heroic

feast *n.* meal, banquet, festival, fête, holiday, anniversary

feat *n.* deed, exploit, achievement, accomplishment, attainment

feature *n.* outstanding part, characteristic quality

feeble *a.* weak, slight, puny, delicate, frail, exhausted, languid, listless

feel *v.* 1. touch, contact, handle, grope
2. be moved/affected/touched

feeling *n.* touch, sense of touch, sensation, emotion, thought

feminine *a.* female, womanly, ladylike, soft, tender, gentle

fence *n.* boundary, bar, barrier, rail, railing, barricade, hedge
v. 1. enclose, encircle, engage
2. evade, prevaricate

ferocious *a.* fierce, savage, wild, untamed, brutal, bestial, barbarous, cruel

fertile *a.* not barren, viable, rich, productive, fruitful, cultivated, fecund

fetch *n.* bring, carry, transport, obtain, get

feud *n.* perpetual quarrel/battle/hostility/dispute

fever *n.* 1. eagerness, excitement, passion
2. illness, sickness, disease

fidget *v.* fret, fuss, be restless/ill at ease, toss, turn

field *n.* 1. land, area, range
2. battlefield, battleground, sportsground

fierce *a.* ferocious, savage, wild, furious, fiery

fight *n.* struggle, combat, battle, action, contest, fray, encounter

figure *n.* 1. shape, outline, form, pattern, body, image
2. digit, number

fill *v.* become full, pack, store, stuff, pour/put in, satiate

final *a.* end, last, terminal, concluding

finale *n.* end, finish, conclusion

find *v.* discover, detect, recover, search/look for

fine *a.* 1. very thin, delicate, of good quality
2. handsome, choice, excellent
3. dry, clear, sunny, bright
n. penalty, forfeit

finish *v.* end, finalize, terminate, conclude, complete, close

firm *a.* fixed, stable, steady, sturdy, solid, hard, tight, secure, steadfast, determined, resolute, adamant

fit *v.* agree, suit, match, be right/proper/appropriate/apt/suitable
n. seizure, spasm, bout, whim, notion

fix *v.* 1. fasten, join, attach, secure
2. mend, repair, adjust
3. decide, arrange, settle, determine
n. problem, difficulty, predicament

flabby *a.* limp, slack, soft, loose, flaccid, fleshy, fat

flake *n.* scale, shaving, tuft

flame *v.* 1. blaze, flare, burn, be on fire
2. be eager/enthusiastic/zealous/passionate
3. be angry/annoyed/in a temper

flash *n.* 1. gleam, glow, light, flare, sparkle
2. instant, moment, second

flat *a.* 1. level, horizontal, even, smooth
2. tasteless, stale, dull, insipid

flavor *n.* taste, relish, piquancy
v. season, salt, add herbs/spices/condiments, spice

flaw *n.* defect, imperfection, fault, weakness

flawless *a.* without defects, perfect

flee *v.* run away, escape, depart hurriedly, fly

flexible *a.* springy, elastic, stretchy, supple, pliant, pliable, resilient

flicker *v.* flutter, waver, quiver, quaver, shake, twitch, fluctuate, shimmer, flare, flash

flight *n.* 1. escape, rapid departure
2. air transport, journey by air/airplane, trajectory, glide
flight of steps: *stairs, stairway, staircase*

fling *v.* hurl, throw, cast, toss, project, heave, pitch

float *v.* drift, hover, sail, be afloat/buoyant

flock *n.* group, herd, gathering, congregation, assembly, crowd, company, throng, followers, adherents

flourish *v.* 1. do well, thrive, succeed, prosper
2. brandish, wave about

flow *v.* pour out, stream, course, gush, flood, run, glide

fluster *v.* upset, confuse, flurry, flutter, bustle, fuss, bother, agitate

fly *v.* 1. flee, escape, run away
2. be in flight, take/make an air journey, soar, wing, glide

foe *n.* enemy, adversary, opponent, antagonist, rival

foggy *a.* misty, cloudy, murky, blurred, hazy, nebulous, vague, dim, unsure, unclear, obscure

folk *n.* people, persons, kin, kith, kindred, kinfolk, relations, relatives, tribe, race

follow *v.* 1. pursue, hunt, chase, run/come/go after, track, trace
2. copy, imitate
3. support, adhere to, observe
4. understand, comprehend

fond *a.* affectionate, loving, caring, devoted, doting, tender, kind

food *n.* nutriment, nourishment, fare, victuals, eatables, rations

fool *n.* idiot, clown, buffoon, oaf, silly person, simpleton, nitwit, dunce
v. 1. jest, joke, play, clown
2. deceive, hoodwink, dupe, trick, outwit, mislead

foolhardy *a.* reckless, rash, risky, headstrong, impetuous, thoughtless, foolish

foot *n.* bottom, base

forbid *v.* disallow, prohibit, ban, prevent

forbidding *a.* threatening, frightening, menacing, unpleasant, baleful

force *v.* make, compel, drive, induce, oblige
n. strength, power, might, energy, effort

forecast *v.* foresee, foretell, predict, prophesy, presage, portend

foreign *a.* 1. alien, from abroad/another country
2. strange, unknown, unfamiliar, unaccustomed

forget *v.* fail to remember/recall/recollect, overlook

forgive *v.* pardon, excuse, let off, overlook

forlorn *a.* without friends, lonely, friendless, forsaken, deserted, neglected, dejected, woebegone, downcast, unhappy, sad, miserable, woeful

form *n.* shape, outline, figure, body, pattern, plan, design, formation

former *a.* earlier, preceding, previous, foregoing, prior

forsake *v.* desert, abandon, leave, neglect, quit, depart from, vacate, give up, disown, abdicate

fortunate *a.* lucky, favored, prosperous, successful

fortune *n.* 1. luck, fate, chance, lot, destiny
2. wealth, prosperity, riches, success

foul *a.* 1. unfair, distasteful, vulgar, nasty, unpleasant, reprehensible
2. dirty, tainted, blemished, sullied, decayed, filthy, putrefied, unclean, polluted

foundation *n.* 1. bottom, base, groundwork, footing, foot, support
2. institution, establishment, organization

fraction *n.* part, portion, piece, bit, section, division

fracture *v.* break, snap, rupture, split, crack

fragile *a.* easily broken/damaged, breakable, flimsy, weak, delicate, brittle, frail

fragment *n.* small piece/part/fraction, bit, morsel, scrap, chip, splinter

fragrance *n.* perfume, scent, pleasant odor/smell

frantic *a.* desperate, fearful, very agitated, panicky, panicking, frenzied, excited, crazy

free *a.* 1. liberated, at liberty, loose, independent, released, discharged, unfastened
2. open, frank, candid
3. liberal, generous, open-handed, lavish
4. at no charge, gratis

frequent *a.* repeated, numerous, regular, many

frequent *v.* visit often/many times, haunt

fresh *a.* 1. new, recent, novel, different, refreshing
2. brisk, lively, invigorating, bracing, vigorous, healthy
3. inexperienced, green, raw, gullible

fret *v.* 1. worry, be concerned/agitated, fuss, vex, annoy, irritate
2. wear away, erode, corrode

friendly *a.* affectionate, agreeable, sociable, companionable, neighborly, kind, helpful

frighten *v.* make afraid/fearful, terrify, scare, alarm, intimidate

frightful *a.* dreadful, terrible, shocking, awful, fearful, horrid, horrible, ghastly

front *n.* face, foremost part, outside, exterior
v. face, confront, encounter, oppose, defy

frown *v.* scowl, look sour/sullen
frown upon: *disapprove of*

fruitful *a.* fertile, productive, gainful, profitable, rich, abundant

frustrate *v.* thwart, oppose, defeat

fugitive *n.* runaway, escapee

fulfill *v.* carry out, accomplish, achieve, complete, finish, end

full *a.* 1. complete, comprehensive, whole, total, entire
2. filled, occupied with

fun *n.* amusement, entertainment, merriment, gaiety, glee, jollity, mirth, frolic, sport, play

funny *a.* 1. amusing, comical, humorous, mirthful, laughable
2. peculiar, odd, strange, queer, unusual

furious *a.* angry, raging, enraged, irate, infuriated, wild, mad, maddened, flaming, frenzied, violent, fierce, wrathful

furnish *v.* provide, give, equip, supply, outfit

further *a.* additional, more distant

furthermore *adv.* moreover, what is more, besides, also, additionally

fury *n.* rage, frenzy, anger, ire, wrath, ferocity

fuss *v.* bother, worry, fidget, fret

futile *a.* vain, pointless, empty, worthless, unprofitable, unsuccessful

G g

gabble *v.* jabber, gibber, prattle, gab, babble, chatter, speak unintelligibly/excessively/confusedly, be incoherent/inarticulate, talk foolishly/idly/wildly

gadget *n.* device, contrivance, small fitting

gag *v.* 1. silence with a gag
2. choke, retch, strangle
n. joke, trick, comedy situation

gain *v.* obtain, get, acquire, receive, win, come to own/possess, collect, glean, achieve, attain, procure

gallant *a.* brave, bold, daring, dashing, courageous, unafraid, fearless, valiant, valorous, dauntless, undaunted, heroic

gallery *n.* long corridor/hall, portico, colonnade, platform, theater balcony, room for an art exhibition

gamble *v.* bet, wager, back, take risks

game *n.* 1. sport, play, amusement, fun, athletic contest, match
2. scheme, undertaking, plan, project, dodge, trick
3. quarry, wild animal (hunted for food), prey
a. 1. brave, bold, daring, plucky, willing, spirited
2. crippled, injured

gang *n.* crew, group, crowd, mob, company, band, troop

gangster *n.* member of a criminal gang, mobster, racketeer, bandit, ruffian, criminal

garment *n.* piece/item of apparel/clothing, item of dress

gasp *v.* gulp, pant, breathe with difficulty

gather *v.* assemble, collect, pick up, crop, reap, glean, combine, meet, congregate, convene

gaudy *a.* showy, flashy, garish, glaring, glossy, loud, lurid

gauge *v.* measure, estimate, assess, standardize, make uniform

gaunt *a.* lean, haggard, grim, cadaverous

gay *a.* joyful, joyous, happy, jolly, cheerful, merry, light-hearted, mirthful, carefree, sporting, playful, full of fun, gleeful, elated

gaze *v.* look at, regard intently/piercingly/fixedly

gear *n.* 1. equipment, apparatus, tools, appliances, tackle, harness, clothing, apparel
2. cog, toothed wheel

gem *n.* jewel, precious stone

general *a.* common, usual, ordinary, normal, standard, customary, widespread, not limited/particular/localized

generous *a.* 1. liberal, freely-giving, magnanimous, munificent, not mean, unprejudiced
2. ample, abundant, copious, fertile, plentiful, plenteous

genial *a.* cordial, jovial, friendly, pleasant, cheerful, sociable, kindly, agreeable, mild, warm, equable, enlivening

gentle *a.* 1. soft, tender, light, mild, kind, quiet, tame, timid, moderate, gradual, manageable
2. genteel, wellborn, of gentle birth, honorable

genuine *a.* real, true, not false/counterfeit/forged, authentic, sound, aboveboard, straight, pure, pedigree, purebred

germinate *v.* begin to grow, shoot, sprout, bud

gesture *n.* 1. meaningful/significant movement of body/limb
2. indication/token of (some kind of emotion)

get *v.* gain, obtain, acquire, receive, win, come to own/possess, collect, glean, achieve, attain

ghastly *a.* 1. pale, wan, white, lurid, ghostlike, unearthly, weird
2. horrible, frightful, dreadful, terrible, shocking, gruesome, grisly, hideous, repulsive, objectionable

ghost *n.* spirit, phantom, spectre, spook, wraith, soul, hallucination, apparition, vision, image

giant *a.* gigantic, unusually large/big/tall, great, huge, mammoth, immense, enormous, tremendous, monstrous, colossal

giddy *a.* 1. dizzy, dazed, faint, inclined to fall/stagger, intoxicated
2. frivolous, flighty, fickle, excitable, inconstant

gift *n.* 1. present, donation, deposit, bestowal, contribution, endowment, benefit, grant, allowance
2. talent, faculty, virtue

gigantic *a.* giant, massive, very big, great, huge, vast, tremendous, enormous, monstrous

give *v.* 1. present, donate, bestow, contribute, endow, grant, award, allow, deliver, hand/make over, impart, confer, devote, dedicate, provide, allot, assign, hold out
2. collapse, break, bend, yield

glad *a.* 1. pleased, happy, content, delighted, joyful
2. bright, beautiful, pleasing, happy, cheerful, joyous, festive

glamorous *a.* beautiful, pretty, attractive, charming, alluring, enchanting, bewitching

glance *n.* quick/momentary look, glimpse, flash, gleam, shaft
v. slide/glide/dart/bounce off, ricochet

glare *n.* 1. dazzle, gleam, flash, fierce/bright light/flame/glow
2. fierce/fixed/angry look

gleam *n.* light, flash, dazzle, beam, flame, glow

glimpse *n.* quick/momentary look, glance

glisten *v.* shine, glitter, gleam, sparkle, flash, twinkle, shimmer

globe *n.* ball, orb, sphere, spheroid
globule: *small ball, spheroid*

gloomy *a.* sad, cheerless, dull, glum, depressed, depressing, unhappy, dismal, downcast, dejected, melancholy, despondent, mournful, threatening, pessimistic, sullen, dark, dusky, dreary, cheerless, drab, not lit/illuminated

glorious *a.* delightful, splendid, wonderful, marvelous, magnificent, brilliant, famous, illustrious, praiseworthy, honorable

glossy *a.* shiny, gleaming, flashy, gaudy, garish

glow *v.* 1. burn brightly, give/throw out light, emit light, incandescence
2. flush, blush, burn with ardor/passion, tingle

glue *n.* gum, paste, adhesive, fixative, mucilage, cement

glum *a.* sad, unhappy, dismal, gloomy, melancholy, downcast, dejected, cheerless, depressed, despondent, pessimistic

glutton *n.* greedy person, excessive eater, person with a great appetite, gourmand, voracious animal

go *v.* 1. move/depart from, start, move off/away
2. journey, travel, proceed, progress, make way, pass into
3. pass, elapse
4. belong
5. be in motion/active/in action

goal *n.* aim, ambition, object, objective, intent, intention, target, purpose

good *a.* 1. true, right, just, kind, gentle, saintly, worthy, virtuous, not corrupted, upright, righteous, generous, benevolent, philanthropic, superior, praiseworthy
2. favorable, beneficial, helpful, sound, wholesome, reliable, dependable, efficient, profitable, unadulterated, fresh, unblemished, untainted
3. skillful, talented, clever, able
n. welfare, betterment, advantage, interest

goods *n.* 1. things owned, belongings, property
2. things for sale, merchandise, wares

gorge *n.* pass, narrow opening/neck between hills/mountains, mountain pass
v. eat/feed/devour greedily, fill, glut, distend, satiate

gorgeous *a.* magnificent, sumptuous, ornate, dazzling, lovely, brilliant, very colorful

gossip *v.* talk idly/lightly/foolishly/unrestrainedly, chatter, prattle, prate, blab, tittle-tattle, spread news/rumors

govern *v.* control, rule, manage, conduct, guide, direct, administer, command, lead, influence, regulate, sway, determine, decide, curb, bridle

grab *v.* seize, snatch, clutch, rip, clasp, grasp, capture, arrest, take/appropriate greedily

graceful *a.* beautiful, beauteous, elegant, refined, charming, well-favored, attractive, pleasing, handsome, ornate

gracious *a.* courteous, polite, well-mannered, mannerly, kind, benevolent, agreeable, pleasing, condescending, indulgent

gradual *a.* slow, not quick/fast/rapid/steep/sudden/abrupt, cautious, by degrees, bit by bit, little by little

grand *a.* great, big, large, elevated, immense, magnificent, splendid, superb, stately, gentlemanly, ladylike, dignified, renowned, celebrated, distinguished, important

grant *v.* give, donate, contribute, present, award, provide, concede, bestow, make available, allow, permit

grasp *v.* 1. seize, grab, snatch, clutch, clasp, grip, hold, take hold of, capture
2. know, understand, comprehend

grateful *a.* thankful, comforting, refreshing, acceptable, favorable, pleasing

great *a.* big, large, grand, huge, vast, immense, gigantic, tremendous, powerful, elevated, important, distinguished, famous, celebra ted, prominent, renowned, well-known, exalted, eminent

greedy *a.* avaricious, covetous, grasping, rapacious, gluttonous, piggish, voracious, ravenous

greet *v.* welcome, salute, hail, acknowledge, bid

grief *n.* 1. sorrow, distress, sadness, woe, misery, heartache, regret, anguish, worry, mourning
2. misfortune, bad luck, trouble, failure, disaster

grip *v.* clutch, grasp, hold, clasp, seize, snatch, grab, capture, arrest

groan *v.* moan, cry with pain/sorrow, whimper, lament, sob, complain, grumble

groove *n.* channel, rut, trench, hollow

gross *a.* 1. big, large, bulky, fat, obese, bloated, overfed
2. glaring, flagrant, palpable
3. total, whole, before/without deductions, not net

ground *n.* earth, floor, base, foundation

group *n.* 1. set, collection, selection, combination, assortment, class, cluster, number, quantity
2. crowd, company, gathering, assembly, gang, throng

grow *v.* 1. get/become bigger/larger, enlarge, increase, expand, swell, amplify, stretch, arise, develop, flourish, spread
2. plant, cultivate, shoot, sprout, germinate, multiply, reproduce, proliferate, mature, ripen

growl *v.* snarl, mutter angrily, grumble, complain

grown-up *a.* grown, adult, mature

gruesome *a.* ghastly, horrible, horrifying, frightening, dreadful, hideous, grim, macabre, grisly, ugly, revolting, unearthly, terrible

grumble *v.* complain, dissent, speak/voice dissent, raise/make objections, growl, murmur, rumble

guarantee *v.* undertake, promise faithfully/truly, warrant, confirm, certify

guess *v.* estimate, suppose, suspect, surmise, imagine, conjecture, hazard, divine
guesswork: *conjecture, supposition*

guide *v.* lead, direct, escort, conduct, advise, counsel, instruct

guile *n.* deceit, treachery, trickery, cunning, slyness, craftiness, artfulness

guilt *n.* crime, sin, wrongdoing, fault, culpability

gullible *a.* easily deceived/tricked/cheated/taken in, too trustful/trusting, innocent, naive (naïve)

gum *n.* glue, paste, adhesive, fixative, cement, mucilage

gun *n.* weapon, firearm, pistol, revolver, automatic, cannon

gush *n.* outrush, fast flow (of liquid), stream
v. make a show of affection/tenderness, speak sentimentally/affectedly

gust *n.* 1. wind, breeze, blast, squall
2. burst of sound/smoke/flame/fire/rain/anger/passion

H h

habit *n.* custom, tradition, practice, rule, routine, procedure, fashion, vogue, mode

habitual *a.* customary, accustomed, usual, normal, regular, general, constant

haggard *a.* careworn, worn-out, gaunt, emaciated, drawn, tired, weary, exhausted, worried troubled

hail *v.* greet, salute, signal, acknowledge, call, shout for, acclaim, applaud, cheer

halt *v.* stop, arrest, hesitate, pause, rest, wait
a. lame, limping, crippled

hammer *v.* beat, knock, strike, pound, hit, drive, bang, rap, tap

hamper *v.* get in the way of, hinder, obstruct, impede, burden, handicap
n. large basket

handicap *n.* disadvantage, hindrance, disability, burden, obstruction, penalty
v. hinder, impede, obstruct, get in the way of, hamper, burden

handle *v.* 1. deal with, undertake, manage, manipulate
2. hold, touch, feel
n. haft, knob

handsome *a.* fair, good-looking, beautiful, lovely, pretty graceful, elegant, comely

handy *a.* 1. near/close by, within reach, useful, helpful, convenient
2. dexterous, adept, skillful, skilled, clever, talented, resourceful

hang *v.* suspend, drape, droop, dangle, swing

haphazard *a.* motley, jumbled, at random, by chance, unplanned

happen *v.* occur, come to pass, take place, chance, befall

happy *a.* delighted, contented, joyful, joyous, bright, glad, pleased, cheerful, cheery, jolly, merry, gleeful, gay, ecstatic, enrapt ured, lucky, fortunate
happy-go-lucky: *easy-going, uncaring, friendly*

harass *v.* pester, plague, annoy, irritate, trouble, bother, badger

hard *a.* 1. firm, solid, strong, unyielding, rigid, durable
2. stern, severe, harsh, unfeeling, insensitive, pitiless, callous, hard-hearted, exacting, unkind, unsympathetic
3. not easy, difficult
hard-headed: *practical, business-like, shrewd, canny*

hardly *adv.* scarcely, with difficulty, only just

hardship *n.* misfortune, mishap, trouble, difficulty, burden, trial, handicap

hardy *a.* strong, sturdy, robust, hearty, vigorous, enduring

harm *v.* hurt, injure, damage, wrong, abuse, treat unfairly/unjustly

harmless *a.* not harmful/hurtful/ damaging, inoffensive, innocent, innocuous

harsh *a.* 1. rough, severe, strict, hard, unfeeling, insensitive, unkind, pitiless, callous, cruel, exacting
2. grating, jarring, rough, unpleasant, unmusical, sharp, piercing

harvest *n.* crop, yield, produce
v. gather, collect, crop

hasty *a.* 1. quick, rapid, speedy, swift, fast
2. abrupt, curt, reckless, rash, impetuous, precipitate, inconsiderate, thoughtless, hurried

hatch *v.* incubate, develop, emerge (from an egg)

hate *v.* dislike, abhor, loathe, detest, be averse to, despise

hateful *a.* detestable, abhorrent, loathsome, distasteful, obnoxious, revolting

haughty *a.* arrogant, overbearing, proud, snobbish, pompous, disdainful

haul *v.* pull, draw, drag, tow
n. catch (of fish), collection, drag, pull

haunt *v.* 1. visit/call frequently
2. follow, chase, dog, hound
n. favorite retreat/den

have *v.* possess, hold, own, secure, obtain, allow, permit, tolerate

hazard *n.* risk, danger, peril, menace, chance, gamble, venture

hazy *a.* 1. misty, cloudy, foggy, dim, dull
2. doubtful, vague, uncertain, indefinite, nebulous, obscure, confused, not clear

head *n.* 1. chief, principal, leader, "boss"
2. source, origin, top, upper end
3. cranium, mind, brain, intelligence

headlong *adv.* 1. head first, head forwards
2. hastily, rashly, recklessly, impetuously, abruptly, thoughtlessly

headstrong *a.* stubborn, obstinate, rash, reckless, willful, hot-headed

heal *v.* cure, treat, restore/bring back to health, mend, repair, remedy

healthy *a.* well, fit, strong, robust, vigorous, hearty, sound, wholesome, salubrious

heap *n.* pile, mound, stack, mass, load, collection, accumulation

hear *v.* listen to, give audience to

heart *n.* center, middle, core, crux, kernel

heartless *a.* unfeeling, insensitive, indifferent, uncaring, pitiless, callous, cruel, unkind, hard-hearted, exacting

hearty *a.* 1. cordial, jovial, genial, friendly, good-natured, cheery, cheerful
2. honest, true, sincere, not hypocritical
3. strong, robust, sturdy

heat *n.* 1. hotness, warmth, glow
2. anger, fury, annoyance
3. excitement, zeal, enthusiasm

heavy *a.* 1. weighty, massive, ponderous, burdensome, cumbersome, sluggish, unyielding, laborious
2. dull, downcast, gloomy, oppressive

hectic *a.* feverish, exciting, bustling, busy, panicky

hedge *n.* fence, barrier, enclosure
v. dodge, evade, avoid, prevaricate

heed *v.* notice, regard, attend, take note of, observe

hefty *a.* heavy, big, large, strong, powerful

help *v.* aid, assist, succor, support

herald *n.* messenger, announcer, forerunner
v. proclaim, announce, usher in

heroic *a.* brave, courageous, valiant, bold, fearless, gallant, daring, undaunted

hesitate *v.* pause, waver, be reluctant, vacillate, falter, demur

hide *v.* conceal, keep secret, cover, lurk, dissemble, disguise
n. skin, pelt

hideous *a.* ugly, horrible, horrid, revolting, frightful, ghastly

high *a.* 1. tall, steep, lofty, elevated
2. exalted, eminent
3. strong, shrill, keen
high-handed: *arrogant, overbearing*
high-minded: *noble, proud*

hilarious *a.* funny, amusing, jolly, merry, gay

hill *n.* small mountain, mount, mound, hillock

hinder *v.* hamper, impede, delay, trammel, handicap, obstruct, block, check, stop

hindmost *a.* last, end, rear, final

hint *n.* roundabout/indirect suggestion, clue, inkling, implication

hire *v.* employ (a person for wages), lend (a thing for a payment), engage, set on

hit *v.* strike, beat, punch, thump, slap, clout, rap, tap, knock, hit, cuff, buffet

hitch *v.* fasten, tie up, attach, tether
n. 1. fastening, tethering, tie
2. difficulty, problem, check, obstruction, hindrance

hoard *n.* hidden/reserve store, hidden treasure, stockpile, collection, accumulation

hoarse *a.* husky, gruff, harsh

hoax *v.* trick, fool, deceive, defraud, bamboozle, spoof, hoodwink, cheat

hold *v.* 1. grasp, grab, clasp, seize, arrest, secure, slop
2. have, own, possess
3. believe, declare, proclaim

hole *n.* 1. hollow, pit, cavity, indentation, bore, space
2. difficulty, fix, mess

holiday *n.* vacation, rest, excursion, leave, anniversary, furlough

hollow *a.* 1. empty, not solid
2. not sincere, insincere, shallow, hypocritical, pretentious
n. hole, pit, cavity, indentation, concavity, crease, wrinkle, furrow, dell, valley

holy *a.* sacred, godly, revered, consecrated, blessed, divine, religious, devout, venerated

home *n.* dwelling, residence, abode

homely *a.* plain, simple, ordinary, commonplace, primitive, unpretentious, uncomely, not comely, homespun

honest *a.* true, upright, straight, open, aboveboard, straightforward, truthful, trustworthy, sincere, honorable, just, fair

honor *n.* good/sound/high/worthy reputation/rank, respect, esteem, renown, fame, glory

hoodwink *v.* cheat, deceive, trick, hoax, fool, bamboozle

hope *v.* expect, anticipate, wish, be ambitious

hopeless *a.* without hope, desperate, despairing, unpromising, impossible

horrible *a.* horrid, terrible, dreadful, hideous, awful, frightful, repulsive, loathsome, repugnant

horrify *v.* frighten, make afraid, shock, dismay, alarm, fill with dread/terror

hospitable *a.* kind, friendly, generous, accommodating, sociable, neighborly

host *n.* 1. multitude, large crowd, swarm, army
2. hotel-keeper, innkeeper
3. entertainer (of guests)

hostile *a.* unfriendly, threatening, antagonistic, menacing

hot *a.* 1. very warm, burning, glowing, aglow, fiery, blazing, ablaze, flaming, aflame
2. eager, hasty, quick
hot-tempered: *quick-tempered, irascible*

house *n.* dwelling, shelter, abode

house *v.* shelter, protect, hold, contain

however *adv.* but, still, nevertheless, howsoever

hue *n.* tint, shade, color, complexion

hug *v.* clasp, embrace, cuddle, squeeze, press, cling, hold

huge *a.* large, big, great, giant, gigantic, enormous, vast, bulky, immense, monstrous, mammoth, tremendous, colossal

human *n.* human being, man, *Homo Sapiens*

humane *a.* kind, merciful, sympathetic, considerate, compassionate, gentle, tender

humble *a.* meek, modest, unimportant, unpretentious, unassuming, shy, retiring, reticent

humor *n.* 1. amusement, fun
2. whim, fancy
v. pamper, spoil, agree with

hungry *a.* starving, famished, ravenous

hunt *v.* search, chase, course, pursue, track, trail, follow, quest, seek, trace

hurl *v.* throw, fling, eject, project, propel, heave, toss, sting, pitch, cast

hurry *v.* haste, hasten, speed, rush, scurry, dash

hurt *v.* injure, harm, pain, wound, maim, bruise, afflict, offend, grieve

hypocritical *a.* false, deceitful, insincere, two-faced

I i

icy *a.* 1. ice-covered, frozen, frosty, frigid, cold
2. unfriendly, hostile, distant, chilly, cool

idea *n.* thought, notion, fancy, concept, impression, conjecture, plan, design, scheme

ideal *a.* perfect, absolute, visionary, faultless

identical *a.* exactly alike/the same, uniform, equivalent

identify *v.* know, recognize, pick out

idiotic *a.* stupid, foolish, silly, absurd, not sensible, nonsensical, crazy, stupid, irrational, illogical, ridiculous

idle *a.* 1. lazy, sluggish, shiftless, unoccupied, inactive, unemployed
2. empty, vain, useless, pointless
3. uncultivated, unfilled, unused, barren

ignite *v.* set alight/on fire, light, take fire, burn, incinerate

ignorant *a.* without knowledge, uneducated, untutored, not learned, unlearned, uninstructed, illiterate

ignore *v.* disregard, refuse to notice, flout, scorn, pooh-pooh, boycott, cold-shoulder

ill *a.* 1. sick, unwell, ailing, indisposed
2. bad, evil, malignant, malevolent
3. unlucky, unfortunate, unfavorable

ill-advised: *unwise, wrongly advised*
ill at ease: *uneasy, embarrassed, nervous*
ill-disposed: *unfriendly, hostile*
ill-favored: *ugly, plain, not comely*
ill-gotten: *dishonestly obtained*
ill health: *poor health, indisposition*
ill humor: *bad temper, moodiness*
ill-judged: *unwise, not circumspect*
ill-natured: *bad tempered, churlish*
ill will: *hatred, enmity, malevolence*

illegal *a.* unlawful, illegitimate, illicit, criminal, against the law

illness *n.* ill health, poor health, indisposition, sickliness, infirmity

illogical *a.* unreasonable, irrational, absurd

illuminate *v.* 1. light, light up, shine upon, throw/cast light upon, brighten
2. enlighten

illusion *n.* deception, image, fantasy, dream, delusion

illustration *n.* 1. picture, drawing
2. example, instance, case, specimen, model

imaginary *a.* not real, unreal, fanciful, fancied, pretended, make-believe, theoretical, hypothetical

imagine *v.* suppose, pretend, fancy, make believe

imitate *v.* copy, match, follow, reproduce, duplicate, mimic, ape, mock, impersonate

immediately *adv.* now, at this time, promptly, without delay instantly, right away, at once, this instant, directly

immense *a.* very large, great, enormous, huge, giant, gigantic, immense, tremendous, vast, mighty, colossal, monstrous

immerse *v.* 1. submerge, plunge, dip sink, douse, soak
2. be absorbed/engrossed in (a book)

imminent *a.* approaching, impending, threatening

immortal *a.* undying, abiding, permanent, everlasting, eternal

immovable *a.* 1. fixed, rigid, solid, immobile
2. stubborn, obstinate, steadfast, resolute

impact *n.* collision, contact, clash

impart *v.* 1. give, donate, make available, convey
2. tell, reveal, inform, instruct, advise

impartial *a.* fair, just, unbiased, unprejudiced

impatient *a.* not patient, restless, fidgety, fretful, fussy, eager, peevish, petulant

impede *v.* hinder, handicap, hamper, restrict, obstruct, delay, oppose, block, check, arrest, frustrate, thwart, retard

imperfect *a.* incomplete, faulty, defective, blemished, tainted, damaged

impertinent *a.* cheeky, saucy, audacious, impudent, forward, rude, bold, impolite, discourteous, brazen, insolent

impetuous *a.* hasty, rash, reckless, abrupt, precipitate, unthinking, headstrong

implore *v.* beg, beseech, entreat, pray

imply *v.* hint, suggest, give a clue/inkling, infer

impolite *a.* rude, discourteous, uncivil, unmannerly, bad-mannered, ill-mannered, disrespectful, impertinent, cheeky, saucy, impudent

important *a.* 1. significant, of moment/consequence, essential, urgent, vital, imperative, pressing, outstanding, momentous, memorable
2. illustrious, notable, prominent, famous, celebrated, eminent

impose *v.* put/place/lay on/upon, tax, take advantage

imposing *a.* great, grand, fine, impressive, awe-inspiring, awesome, striking, splendid, mighty, majestic, noble, stately

impressive *a.* great, imposing, awe-inspiring, awesome, striking, stirring, moving, thrilling, exciting, notable

impromptu *a.* unprepared, unrehearsed, off-hand, spontaneous

improper *a.* not proper/correct, wrong, incorrect, unsuitable, unsatisfactory, unbecoming, indecent, unseemly

improve *v.* make/become better, amend

imprudent *a.* unwise, ill-advised, rash, reckless

impudent *a.* audacious, impertinent, cheeky, saucy, rude, forward, disrespectful, brazen, bold, flippant

impulsive *a.* impatient, hasty, reckless, rash, impetuous, precipitate, unthinking, thoughtless, careless

impure *a.* not pure, adulterated, unclean, tainted, foul, dirty

inadequate *a.* unsatisfactory, insufficient, unsuitable, deficient

inappropriate *a.* unsuitable, inadequate, unsatisfactory, unbecoming, improper, unseemly

incessant *a.* unceasing, without ceasing, continual, constant, unending, endless, perpetual, ceaseless, eternal

incident *n.* event, happening, occurrence, affair, occasion, episode

incompetent *a.* incapable, unqualified, unfit, deficient

incorrect *a.* wrong, unsuitable, faulty, unsatisfactory, inappropriate, inadequate, inaccurate, erroneous, improper

increase *v.* make/become larger/greater, enlarge, grow, multiply, gain, extend, expand, swell, raise

incredible *a.* surprising, amazing, astounding, hard to believe/accept/understand

indecent *a.* coarse, disgusting, rude, vulgar, uncouth, improper, unseemly, unbecoming

indeed *adv.* in truth/reality, really, truly, for certain, certainly

indefinite *a.* uncertain, unsure, vague, ambiguous, undecided, undefined, unfixed, unclear

independent *a.* free, at liberty, alone, uncontrolled, separate, self-sufficient, self-reliant

indicate *v.* point out, show, mark, hint, tell, designate

indifferent *a.* 1. uninterested, unconcerned, tolerant
2. mediocre, moderate, passable

indignation *n.* resentment, anger, annoyance

indirect *a.* not direct, roundabout, circuitous

indispensable *a.* essential, necessary, much needed, required

indistinct *a.* dim, dull, blurred, misty, hazy, nebulous, vague, uncertain, confused, indefinite, obscure

industrious *a.* busy, hard-working, active, diligent

ineffective *a.* useless, vain, idle, powerless, ineffectual, inadequate

inevitable *a.* certain, sure, inescapable, unavoidable

inferior *a.* 1. lower, below
2. poor, poorer, mediocre, second-rate

infinite *a.* boundless, limitless, endless, countless, immeasurable, unlimited, eternal, immense

infirm *a.* 1. feeble, frail, weak, ailing
2. unsound, unstable

inflame *v.* set alight/ablaze

inflate *v.* expand, distend, swell, dilate, puff up

influence *v.* affect, sway, persuade, direct, control, guide, lead

inform *v.* tell, make known to, advise

infrequent *a.* irregular, unusual, uncommon, rare

infuriate *v.* anger, vex, annoy, enrage, make furious, madden, incense, inflame

ingenious *a.* clever, gifted, talented, skillful, inventive

inhabit *v.* live/abide/reside/dwell/stay/lodge in, occupy

inhuman *a.* not human/like a human, brutal, bestial, inhumane

injure *v.* hurt, harm, maim, wound, damage

inkling *n.* suggestion, hint, whisper, suspicion

innocent *a.* without guilt/fault, not guilty/at fault, guiltless, faultless, blameless, harmless, innocuous, naïve (naive)

inquire *v.* ask, question, investigate, seek knowledge

inquisitive *a.* curious, inquiring, prying

insecure *a.* unsafe, unguarded

insignificant *a.* little, small, trivial, petty, trifling, unimportant, of no consequence, inconsequential

insolent *a.* impudent, impertinent, cheeky, saucy, rude, insulting, offensive, defiant

inspect *v.* examine, check, investigate

instant *a.* urgent, pressing, prompt, immediate
n. moment, present month/time

instruct *v.* 1. teach, train, coach, tutor
2. order, command, direct, guide, inform, tell, advise

insufficient *a.* inadequate, scanty, meager, not enough

insult *v.* offend, cheek, abuse, be insolent/impertinent/impudent/rude to

intact *a.* 1. complete, whole, perfect, sound
2. undamaged, unhurt, uninjured, unharmed, unbroken

intelligent *a.* sensible, alert, shrewd, astute, well-informed

intention *n.* intent, aim, purpose, goal, object, plan, idea, motive

intentional *a.* intended, deliberate, premeditated

internal *a.* inner, inside, interior

interval *n.* pause, gap, break, recess

intricate *a.* complicated, complex, involved, tricky, difficult

intrude *v.* enter uninvited, encroach, invade

invade *v.* intrude, enter, encroach

invasion *n.* encroachment, intrusion

invalid *a.* valueless, worthless

invalid *n.* sick/ailing/convalescent person

invent *v.* devise, make up, create, concoct, design, conceive, fabricate, plan, fashion, discover, originate

investigate *v.* inquire into, ask/question about, inspect, examine, check, search

irate *a.* angry, annoyed, vexed, furious, enraged

irksome *a.* tedious, tiresome, wearisome, boring, frustrating, irritating, perturbing

irritable *a.* fretful, peevish, petulant, easily annoyed/vexed/exasperated

irritate *v.* 1. annoy, vex, exasperate, aggravate, provoke, bother, trouble, disturb
2. itch, chafe, make sore

J j

jab *n.* poke, stab, thrust, hit, abrupt/sudden/sharp/quick blow, punch

jabber *v.* chatter, babble, gab, gabble, gibber, speak/talk quickly/ incessantly/wildly/ senselessly/foolishly/ incoherently

jade *v.* tire, fatigue, wear out, make feel inferior
a. She felt quite **jaded** at the end of the day's work.

jagged *a.* rough, rough-edged, coarse, barbed, toothed, notched, crooked

jail *n.* prison, penitentiary, reformatory, dungeon

jam *v.* squeeze, crush, wedge in, crowd tightly together, block, fill up, make a stoppage, cram
n. 1. squeeze, crush, blockage, stoppage, crowd
2. conserve, preserve, confection

jangle *v.* sound harshly/noisily, clatter, clank, make bell-like sounds

jar *v.* jolt, grate, scrape, shake, bump, jerk, push, knock, move, jiggle, joggle, jostle, vibrate, throb, resound, sound harshly/discordantly, send shocks through
n. pot, urn, vase, pitcher, jug, vessel

jaunt *n.* outing, excursion, expedition, journey for pleasure
We took a **jaunt** to the beach in August.

jealous *a.* envious, grudging, resentful, distrustful, mistrustful, suspicious, intolerant

jeer *v.* sneer, taunt, gibe (jibe), deride, scoff, mock, make fun of, poke fun at, laugh at, joke about, ridicule, chaff, flout

jerk *v.* yank, pull, push, tug, thrust, nudge, snatch, jump, jolt, jig, jiggle, jog, joggle, twist, twitch, tremble, vibrate, move

jest *v.* joke, banter, taunt, scoff, chaff, ridicule, make/poke fun, quip, gag, speak/act amusingly/playfully/ funnily/comically/with humor, trifle

jewel *n.* 1. precious stone, gem
2. invaluable/precious/useful/ greatly loved/much esteemed person/thing

jig *n.* brisk/quick/rapid/lively dance, jump, skip, gallop, up-and-down movement/ motion, jog, jiggle, shake

jingle *n.* 1. tinkle, clink, bell-like sound, chain-like noise, jangle
2. little/popular/well-known/ easily-remembered/lively rhyme

jittery *a.* nervous, afraid, fearful, frightened, scared, timid, jumpy, worried, anxious, apprehensive

job *n.* 1. task, piece of work
2. business, employment, occupation, profession, post, trade, work, vocation

jog *v.* 1. shake, push, jerk, jolt, nudge, thrust
2. jig, dance, trot, trudge, walk unsteadily, travel slowly, go forward laboriously

join *v.* 1. unite, combine, fasten, blend, merge, amalgamate, bind, marry
2. enroll, participate, enter

joke *v.* jest, gag, banter, quip, gibe (jibe), make/poke fun, banter, chaff, scoff, speak/act amusingly/with humor/playfully/funnily/ comically, trifle

jolly *a.* cheerful, happy, gay, joyful, joyous, mirthful, merry, festive, jovial, jocular, full of fun, amusing, lively, plea.sant

jolt *n.* jerk, bump, sudden/ abrupt/sharp blow, knock, jog, nudge

jot *n.* trifle, dot, tiny fragment
v. write down, make quick/rough notes

journey *n.* trip, voyage, expedition, excursion, distance travelled/traversed

jovial *a.* cheerful, happy, gay, merry, mirthful, jocular, good-humored, good-natured, full of fun, pleasant, festive

joy *n.* delight, happiness, joyfulness, joyousness, merriment, glee, jubilance, gladness, felicity, jollity, bliss, great pleasure, jubilation

jubilant *a.* joyful, delighted, glad, very happy, rejoicing, exultant. triumphant

judge *v.* assess, estimate, decide, form opinion about, suppose, consider, form/ make/give judgement, criticize, censure, act as a judge, try, adjudicate, pass sentence on

jumble *v.* mix up, muddle, confuse, disarrange, disarray, throw into disorder
n. junk, oddments, discarded clothes/objects

jump *v.* leap, spring, skip, gambol, jig, jog, move up and down, start, move, wince, twitch, shake, jolt, jerk

junk *n.* jumble, oddments, waste, rubbish, discarded objects

just *a.* fair, impartial, right, true, aboveboard, honest, straight, correct, proper, suitable, fitting, deserved, equitable, righteous, upright
adv. exactly, precisely, truly, quite, barely, only, then, at that time, now, at this time, very recently

justice *n.* 1. fairness, rightness, impartiality, fair treatment, just conduct, equity, lawful/legal authority
2. magistrate, judge

jut *v.* stick out, project, protrude

juvenile *n.* child, youngster, young person, minor

K k

keen *a.* 1. sharp, sharp-edged, cutting, piercing, biting, bitter, penetrating, acute, quick, quick-witted, alert, sensitive, intense, vivid, acute
2. zealous, enthusiastic, willing, eager, ardent, fervent, earnest, much interested, zestful, vigorous, active, busy, industrious

keep *v.* hold, retain, save, possess, look after, preserve, guard, maintain, protect, detain, reserve, have charge of, adhere to, observe, pay regard to, be true to, stand by, remain, stay

kidnap *v.* abduct, carry off by force, take away (a person), steal (a child)

kill *v.* murder, slay, slaughter, massacre, butcher, put to death, put an end to, cause the death of, harm fatally/mortally, destroy, liquidate, execute, assassinate, exterminate

kin *n.* kindred, kinsfolk, kith, family, relatives, relations, group, tribe, race
akin: *alike, similar, of the same group/tribe/race*

kind *n.* type, sort, variety, quality, character, nature, category, class, classification, group, family, kin, kindred, tribe, race
a. kind-hearted, considerate, thoughtful, gentle, tender, loving, affectionate, friendly, benevolent, philanthropic, good, courteous

king *n.* ruler, monarch, sovereign, His Majesty

kingdom *n.* realm, domain, dominion

kit *n.* set, outfit, equipment, tools, apparatus

knack *n.* art, skill, dexterity, ability, faculty, cleverness, trick, habit, method, means, technique

knock *v.* strike, rap on/at, hit, tap
n. punch, bump, bang, thud

knot *v.* tie, tangle, rope together, link, join, unite, marry

know *v.* 1. have knowledge of, be aware of, understand, comprehend, realize, have learned, be versed in, be informed about
2. be acquainted with, be intimate with, recognize, be able to distinguish, identify, be certain/sure of
know-it-all: *one who professes/pretends to know everything*
know-how: *special skill, expertise*

knowing *a.* knowledgeable, well-informed, shrewd, astute, cunning, artful, sharp, wide-awake, cute, intelligent, clever

knowledge *n.* learning, understanding, information, intelligence, experience

L l

label *n.* 1. title, name, mark, stamp
2. tag, seal

labor *n.* work, toil, task, effort, exertion, industry, employment

laborious *a.* tiring, fatiguing, wearisome, toilsome, exhausting, exacting, painstaking, hard, heavy, tough, difficult, industrious, diligent

lack *v.* be without, be deprived/ deficient in, short/in want of, require, need

lag *v.* linger, dawdle, loiter, straggle, delay

lame *a.* 1. limping, crippled, injured
2. unsatisfactory, poor, inadequate, imperfect

land *n.* 1. earth, ground
2. country, territory, region
3. estate, farm, holding
v. get/go ashore/on shore/land, beach

large *a.* big, great, grand, huge, enormous, massive, giant, gigantic, bulky, vast, spacious, monstrous, abundant, ample, plentiful

last *a.* 1. end, final, hindmost, terminal, concluding
2. latest, most recent
v. hold out, endure, persist, stay, remain

lasting *a.* enduring, permanent, perpetual, durable, stable, steady, constant

late *a.* 1. behind time, overdue, tardy, delayed, slow
2. deceased, departed, dead
3. past, recent

laugh *v.* guffaw, chuckle, exult, scoff
laugh at: *make fun of, ridicule, scoff at*

laughable *a.* amusing, funny, comic, comical, mirth-provoking, humorous

lavish *a.* liberal, generous, extravagant, open-handed, munificent, bountiful

lawful *a.* legal, legitimate, permissible, permitted/ allowed by law

lawless *a.* disorderly, unruly, rebellious, uncontrollable, uncontrolled, unmanageable

lax *a.* easy, easy-going, loose, slack, negligent, careless, unmindful

layer *n.* film, deposit, stratum, seam, thickness

lazy *a.* idle, indolent, sluggish, lethargic, slothful

lead *v.* 1. guide, conduct, escort, control, direct, steer, command
2. excel, surpass, be in front/advance/ahead

leader *n.* guide, head, chief, captain, commander, director, conductor, controller, master, boss

leak *v.* escape, run/pass/flow out, come out slowly/gradually, transpire

lean *v.* incline, slant, slope, bend, rest
a. thin, lank, lanky, slender, skinny

leap *v.* jump, spring, bound, vault, skip, gambol, caper

learned *a.* wise, well-informed, scholarly, well-educated

learning *n.* knowledge, education, scholarship

leave *v.* 1. depart, quit, go away/out, vacate, desert, forsake
2. will, bequeath
n. 1. permission, consent
2. holiday, absence, vacation, furlough

left *a.* left-hand, left-hand side

legal *a.* lawful, legitimate, allowed/permitted by law, permissible

legend *n.* story, tale, myth, fable, fiction

legendary *a.* mythical, fabulous, fanciful, fictitious, imaginary, marvelous, wonderful

legitimate *a.* 1. lawful, legal, allowed/permitted by law, permissible
2. true, real, authentic, proper, genuine, regular, acceptable, admissible

leisure *n.* spare/free time, ease, comfort, relaxation, rest

lengthen *v.* make longer, stretch, extend, increase

lenient *a.* mild, gentle, easy, easygoing, merciful

lessen *v.* lower, diminish, reduce, shorten, decrease

let *v.* allow, permit, tolerate

level *a.* flat, horizontal, even, smooth, straight, regular
v. knock down, raze, demolish

liberate *v.* set free/loose, release, give freedom to, discharge

lie *v.* 1. lay, rest, recline, be recumbent
2. tell an untruth/falsehood, fib, dissemble

lift *v.* raise, hoist, elevate
n. help, aid, assistance, support

light *v.* illuminate, ignite, set/on fire, afire
a. gentle, flimsy, frail, of little weight

lighten *v.* 1. light up, brighten, clear, illuminate
2. lessen/reduce/diminish load/burden/weight, make less heavy, ease, relieve

like *v.* love, approve of, be pleased with
a. alike, similar, resembling

limit *n.* border, boundary, edge, barrier, restriction, check, restraint, end, curtailment, curb, control

limp *a.* not stiff/rigid, flabby, slack, flaccid, drooping, loose, lax
v. walk awkwardly/lamely

linger *v.* delay, hang about, persist, tarry, dawdle, loiter, dally, lag

link *v.* connect, join, attach, bind, tie, unite, couple, knot, fasten, fix

list *n.* roll, register, record, inventory, tally, catalog, manifest, table
v. lean to one side

listen *v.* hear, attend

listless *a.* weary, tired, fatigued, slack, limp, languid, feeble, drooping

litter *n.* jumble, rubbish, waste, refuse

little *a.* small, tiny, diminutive, wee, minute
n. small quantity/amount/piece, morsel, bit, scrap
adv. not much/a lot, slightly

live *v.* 1. exist, be alive
2. dwell, reside, stay, remain, lodge, inhabit, abide

live *a.* 1. active, viable
2. glowing, unexploded

lively *a.* 1. active, brisk, nimble, alive, spritely, vigorous, spirited
2. cheerful, gay, jolly, merry, joyful, bright, brilliant, vivid

loath *a.* unwilling, reluctant

loathe *v.* hate, abhor, dislike intensely, detest, despise

locate *v.* place, put, site, situate

lofty *a.* 1. high, elevated, towering
2. conceited, haughty, proud, aloof

loiter *v.* hang about, linger, dawdle, dally, delay, lag, tarry

lonely *a.* lone, alone, lonesome, forlorn, companionless, isolated, desolate

long *a.* lengthy, extended, prolonged, far-reaching
v. desire, yearn, crave

look *v.* 1. regard, observe, behold, eye, watch, examine, inspect, peep, glance, view, stare, gaze
2. search, seek
3. seem, appear

lose *v.* 1. miss, mislay, drop
2. fail, be defeated/beaten/unsuccessful

lot *n.* 1. all, every one, total number/quantity/amount, much, many
2. item, article
3. luck, fortune, fate, chance, destiny

loud *a.* 1. noisy, blaring, deafening, discordant, tumultuous, clamorous, boastful, bombastic
2. gaudy, glossy, vivid, bright, glaring

love *v.* like, hold dear, be fond of, be devoted to, cherish, adore

lovely *a.* beautiful, attractive, charming, pleasing, delightful, fine, lovable

loyalty *n.* faithfulness, devotion, fidelity, constancy

luck *n.* fortune, fate, lot, chance, destiny, success

lucky *a.* fortunate, favored

lull *v.* soothe, quiet, placate, calm

lurk *v.* hide, be concealed, lie in wait, prowl, skulk, sneak

lustrous *a.* bright, shining, radiant, splendid, brilliant, glossy

luxuriant *a.* rich, rank, prolific, profuse, lush, abundant, dense, thick

luxury *n.* costliness, wealth, opulence, affluence

M m

macabre *a.* grim, hideous, grisly, gruesome

mad *a.* 1. insane, mentally ill/sick, deranged, frenzied
2. angry, annoyed, furious, enraged, irate

magazine *n.* 1. warehouse, storehouse, store
2. periodical, journal

magic *n.* 1. witchcraft, wizardry, sorcery, devilry
2. conjuring, legerdemain, sleight-of-hand, juggling

magnificent *a.* grand, superb, splendid, wonderful, marvelous, sumptuous

magnify *v.* make/become larger/bigger/greater, increase, enlarge, expand, exaggerate, amplify

maid *n.* maiden, girl, lass, wench, miss, damsel

mail *n.* 1. postal service, letter post
2. letters, correspondence

maim *v.* injure, wound, disable, cripple, hurt, mutilate, mangle, crush, disfigure

main *a.* principal, most important, chief, central
n. **might and main:** *physical force/strength/power*

maintain *v.* 1. keep, provide for, sustain, uphold, support, preserve
2. claim, hold, insist

majestic *a.* stately, regal, royal, grand, noble, magnificent, splendid, dignified

major *a.* 1. greater, larger, more important, senior, superior
2. army/military officer

majority *n.* 1. greater part/portion/number/fraction, bulk, most
2. adulthood

make *v.* 1. do, perform, create, devise, fabricate, manufacture, construct, erect
2. compel, force
make-believe: *false, sham, pretended, imitation, bogus*

malady *n.* ailment, illness, sickness, disease, fever, ill health, indisposition, complaint

male *n.* man, boy, masculine animal

mammoth *a.* giant, gigantic, huge, immense, enormous, colossal
n. mastodon

man *n.* 1. male, gentleman
2. employee, workman, hand
3. mankind, humanity, human race, *Homo Sapiens*

manage *v.* 1. control, direct, run, organize, regulate, govern, administer
2. make do, get by/along

manageable *a.* controllable, disciplined, orderly, docile, timid, tame, gentle, quiet, obedient

manhood *n.* manliness, adulthood, maturity

mankind *n.* man, humans, humanity, human race

manly *a.* strong, virile, brave, bold, courageous, noble

manner *n.* 1. way, method, approach, technique
2. style, mode, fashion, kind, sort, form

mannerism *n.* habit, trick, style, gesture, distinctive manner

manners *n.* behavior, conduct, habits, courtesy, politeness, etiquette, civility

manual *n.* handbook, instruction book, guide
a. by hand, done with the hands

manufacture *v.* make, construct, produce, fabricate, build

many *a.* a lot of, numerous, plenty, various

map *n.* chart, plan, diagram, outline

march *v.* walk/move in step, pace, pound

margin *n.* edge, border, boundary, rim, brink, limit

marine *a.* sea, nautical, maritime, oceanic

mark *n.* 1. token, sign, indication, symbol, label, imprint, impression, brand, stamp
2. stain, scar, blemish, smudge, speck, spot, blotch
v. 1. observe, pay regard/attention to, attend to, notice, note, watch
2. point at, indicate, label

market *n.* fair, bazaar, store, shops, shopping center

marketable *a.* saleable, commercial

maroon *v.* abandon (e.g., on an uninhabited island), desert, leave behind, isolate

marry *v.* tie, join, unite, bind, wed

marsh *n.* swamp, bog, morass, mire, fen, quagmire, slough

marvelous *a.* wonderful, amazing, extraordinary, unbelievable, delightful, splendid, superb

masculine *a.* male, manly, strong, virile, robust

mask *v.* disguise, hide, conceal, cover

mass *n.* 1. quantity, amount, weight, body, bulk, size
2. crowd, crush, mob

massacre *v.* slaughter, slay, kill, destroy, liquidate, butcher, put to death

massive *a.* ponderous, enormous, very large/big/heavy/bulky, giant, gigantic, huge, unwieldy

master *n.* 1. employer, controller, head, chief, boss, director, leader
2. expert, teacher, instructor
v. overcome, overpower, gain control/command of, subdue, tame, conquer

mastery *n.* control, command, power, supremacy, knowledge, grasp, understanding, skill, proficiency

masticate *v.* chew, grind

mat *n.* small rug/carpet, pad
a. matt, coarse, rough
v. tangle, twist

match *v.* 1. be alike/the same, blend, harmonize, agree, tally, fit
2. equal, overcome, oppose
n. 1. wedding, marriage
2. equal
3. contest, game, competition
4. wooden splint

material *n.* 1. substance, matter
2. facts, information, data
3. cloth, fabric
a. 1. real, actual, substantial, vital, essential, relevant, important
2. worldly, earthly

matter *n.* 1. substance, material
2. happening, occurrence, event, topic, episode, affair, business, question
3. pus
v. count, signify, be relevant/important
matter-of-fact: *calm, down-to-earth, unemotional, nonchalant*

mature *a.* ripe, ready, full-grown, grown-up

maximum *a.* greatest, largest, biggest, most, utmost, supreme, highest

maybe *adv.* perhaps, possibly, by chance
maze
n. labyrinth, puzzle, riddle
v. puzzle, bewilder, baffle, perplex, mystify

meager *a.* poor, small, trifling, slight, slim, scanty, limited, sparse, mean, niggardly

mean *a.* 1. poor, small, meager, scanty, niggardly, trifling, stingy, ungenerous, miserly
2. coarse, common, vulgar, nasty, base, vile, spiteful, unkind
3. middle, average
v. 1. intend, aim
2. signify, indicate, show, convey

meaning *n.* explanation, definition, sense, significance, substance, intention, aim, object, purpose, point

meaningless *a.* without meaning, nonsensical, senseless, absurd, idiotic, pointless, useless

means *n.* 1. method, way, technique, device, artifice, process
2. money, wealth, possessions

measure *v.* determine/find the size of, assess, estimate, gauge
n. 1. estimate, dimension, size
2. measuring-instrument, gauge, ruler

mechanical *a.* 1. machine-like, automatic, robot-like, of machines/machinery
2. blind, unthinking, instinctive

mechanism *n.* machine, works, device

meddle *v.* interfere, pry, tamper, intervene, busybody

meek *a.* mild, timid, tame, docile, gentle, shy, humble, lowly, modest, retiring, reticent, unassuming

meet *v.* 1. encounter, confront, come face to face
2. join, unite, converge, come together, assemble, muster, gather, congregate, convene
3. satisfy, fulfill, fill, answer
a. proper, correct, appropriate

melancholy *a.* sad, unhappy, dismal, gloomy, dejected, sorrowful, depressed, despondent, distressed, mournful, downcast, plaintive, melancholic

mellow *a.* 1. ripe, juicy, soft, sweet, delicate, mature, perfect
2. friendly, sociable, genial, cordial

member *n.* 1. limb, organ, part
2. entrant, affiliate, fellow, associate

memorize *v.* commit to memory, learn by heart

menace *n.* threat, danger, peril, hazard

mend *v.* repair, restore, correct, improve, adjust, rectify, overhaul, fix, patch, sew, stitch, darn

mental *a.* of the mind/brain/intellect, intellectual

mention *v.* name, nominate, speak of/about, refer to, state, declare, tell
n. notice, reference, statement, nomination

merchant *n.* trader, dealer, factor

mercy *n.* forgiveness, leniency, pity, compassion, sympathy, humanity, kindness

merge *v.* come together, join, unite, mix, blend, mingle, combine, be absorbed

merit *v.* deserve, earn, win

merry *a.* happy, gay, carefree, jolly, joyful, festive, jovial, cheerful, hilarious, vivacious

mess *n.* disorder, muddle, mix-up, confusion, jumble, litter, rubbish, dirt

method *n.* 1. way, manner, means, process, technique, approach
2. order, orderliness, system, arrangement

methodical *a.* orderly, systematic, significant, purposeful

middle *a.* mid, midway, mean, central

might *n.* energy, force, power, strength, intensity, vigor, greatness

mild *a.* 1. meek, timid, inoffensive, shy, soft, smooth, gentle, light, calm, placid, easy, kind
2. warm, fine, sunny

military *a.* soldierly, soldier-like, martial
n. army

mime *v.* mimic, imitate

mimic *v.* imitate, copy, ape, mock

mind *n.* brain, intellect, understanding
v. 1. take care of, guard, watch, keep, look after
2. heed, attend/pay regard to, obey
3. remember, recollect, recall
4. object to

mindful *a.* heedful, attentive, observant, aware, watchful

mine *n.* 1. pit, shaft, colliery
2. bomb

miniature *a.* small, tiny, petite, model, toy

minimum *a.* least, smallest, lowest

minor *a.* smaller, lesser, less important, lower, junior
n. juvenile, youngster, child

minority *n.* smaller part/portion/number/fraction, least

minus *a.* less, without, short of, negative

minute *a.* very/extremely small/little/tiny, insignificant

miraculous *a.* marvelous, wonderful, amazing, astounding, astonishing, surprising, magical, divine

mirror *n.* looking-glass, reflector
v. reflect, copy, imitate

mirth *n.* merriment, gaiety, jollity, glee, fun, amusement, laughter, hilarity

miscellaneous *a.* varied, various, mixed, assorted, mingled, diverse, divers, sundry

mischief *n.* 1. naughtiness, willfullness, pranks
2. damage, injury, destruction, vandalism

misconduct *n.* bad conduct/behavior, misbehavior, disorder

miserable *a.* sad, unhappy, gloomy, melancholy, doleful, depressed, dejected, despondent, sorrowful, woeful, mournful

misfortune *n.* bad/ill fortune/luck, difficulty, disaster, calamity

miss *v.* 1. overlook, neglect, skip, lose, omit, leave out, avoid, fail to go/attend/hit
2. notice/regret the loss/absence of
n. girl, young lady/woman, lass, unmarried woman, spinster

mission *n.* task, duty, expedition, errand, assignment, purpose

mist *n.* fog, cloud, haze, moisture, dew, vapor

mistake *n.* error, fault, defect, flaw

mix *v.* combine, blend, mingle, unite, join

mob *n.* crowd, rabble, mass
v. crowd, crush, overwhelm, jostle, molest

mobile *a.* moving, quick, active, movable, portable

mock *a.* sham, imitation, false, fake, counterfeit
v. make fun of, deride, scoff, jeer, laugh at, tease, mimic, imitate

model *n.* 1. example, specimen, prototype, pattern, figure, design
2. small/miniature/toy copy/version
v. make, mold, shape, fashion, form, design, plan

moderate *a.* fair, reasonable, not extreme, restrained

moderate *v.* soothe, pacify, placate, soften, control, reduce, check, curb

modern *a.* new, up-to-date, current, recent

modest *a.* meek, shy, retiring, reticent, humble, unassuming

moist *a.* damp, wet, humid

molest *v.* pester, interfere with, disturb, bother, trouble, annoy, worry

moment *n.* 1. instant, second, flash
2. importance

monarch *n.* ruler, sovereign, king, queen, emperor, empress

monotonous *a.* unchanging, regular, dull, tedious, boring, uninteresting, wearisome

monster *n.* terrifying animal/beast, cruel/barbarous/inhuman man

moody *a.* sullen, sulky, peevish

mope *v.* fret, sulk, be listless/ discontented/dispirited

moral *a.* well-conducted, good, upright, ethical, virtuous, pious, honest, honorable, respectable

morale *n.* spirit, confidence, cheerfulness

moreover *adv.* what is more, furthermore, besides, also, in addition, additionally

morsel *n.* small piece, bit, fragment, shred, scrap

motion *n.* 1. movement, action, disturbance
2. proposal, suggestion

motionless *a.* without motion/action, still, stationary, not moving

mount *v.* 1. climb, go up, rise, ascend, get on, bestride (a horse or bicycle)
2. place, set, fix, display
n. hill, hillock, mound

mourn *v.* grieve, lament, sorrow

move *v.* 1. carry, transfer
2. move place/position, travel, stir, shift
3. touch, arouse, agitate, excite
4. propose, suggest, recommend

n. step, act, action, decision

multiply *v.* increase, make/become greater/more, reproduce

multitude *n.* crowd, throng, mass

murder *v.* kill, slaughter, slay, have put to death, destroy, liquidate

must *v.* should, ought, are compelled/obliged to

musty *a.* stale, moldy, sour, fetid

mutiny *v.* disobey, revolt, rebel, riot
n. revolt, rebellion, uprising

mutter *v.* murmur, mumble, growl, grumble, complain, whisper

mystery *n.* puzzle, enigma, riddle, secret

myth *n.* story, tale, fable, legend

N n

nag *v.* give no peace to, pester, scold/find fault with persistently/regularly, chide, reprove

naked *a.* nude, bare, unclothed, uncovered, undressed, exposed, bald

name *n.* 1. title, label, appellation, term
2. reputation
v. nominate, mention, speak of

nap *n.* short sleep, doze, siesta, snooze

narrate *v.* tell (a story), relate, recount, describe, reveal, make known, state, recite

narrow *a.* 1. thin, not wide/broad, slender, contracted, restricted, limited, cramped
2. prejudiced, biased, narrow-minded, small-minded, petty

nasty *a.* unpleasant, offensive, mean, ill-tempered, disagreeable, spiteful, vindictive, dirty, unclean, filthy, rotten, polluted, foul

native *a.* 1. inborn, inherent
2. natural, uncivilized
n. inhabitant, indigenous animal/plant/person

natural *a.* 1. inborn, inherent, native
2. simple, unaffected, unadorned, usual, normal, lifelike, realistic, unpretentious, unforced

nature *n.* 1. creation, the universe
2. quality, characteristic, manner, kind, sort
3. personality, disposition, character, instinct

naughty *a.* mischievous, misbehaved, badly-behaved, bad, ill-behaved, troublesome, disobedient, willful, wicked

navigate *v.* direct course, cruise, sail, steer, pilot

near *adv.* near by, close, nigh, at/to a short distance, neighboring
a. closely related/connected

nearly *adv.* almost, all but, closely

neat *a.* 1. tidy, clean, orderly, trim, smart, well-groomed
2. adept, deft, adroit
3. pure, unadulterated, unmixed

necessary *a.* needful, essential, required, wanted, needed, indispensable

need *v.* want, require
n. want, lack, poverty, necessity, distress, hardship

needy *a.* in need/want/poverty/ distress, poor, destitute

negative *a.* not positive, contrary, opposite, difficult
v. refuse, forbid, disallow, oppose
n. photographic film/plate
in the negative: *no, not*
He replied in the **negative**, "No, certainly not."

neglect *n.* lack of care, carelessness, indifference, disregard
v. not care for/maintain/look after, miss, omit, ignore, fail, forget

neglectful *a.* careless, thoughtless, indifferent, remiss, negligent, inattentive

negotiate *v.* 1. bargain, haggle, transact, make/arrange terms
2. exchange, transfer, pass over/through

neighborhood *n.* vicinity, locality, district, area

nerve *n.* courage, pluck, daring, resolution, boldness

nervous *a.* nervy, fearful, timid, apprehensive, afraid, uneasy, tense, jumpy, shaky, jittery

net *n.* 1. netting, mesh, grid, network, web
2. snare, trap
v. snare, enmesh, trap, catch, capture
a. not gross, after deductions, real, actual

neutral *a.* neither for nor against, impartial, unbiased, without prejudice

new *a.* 1. previously/hitherto unknown, unfamiliar, strange, different, novel, original
2. recent, latest, fresh, unused

news *n.* information, tidings, bulletin, message, report

next *a.* nearest, adjacent, succeeding, following, after

nice *a.* 1. pleasant, favorable, good, delicious, agreeable, friendly, lovely, charming, delightful, fine, delicate
2. exact, precise, accurate

nil *n.* nothing, nought, zero

nimble *a.* quick, brisk, sprightly, spry, agile, lively, alive, active, alert, quick-witted

nip *v.* bite, pinch, squeeze

noble *a.* worthy, great, distinguished, honorable, eminent, celebrated, illustrious, lordly, dignified, majestic, brave, gallant, dashing
n. lord, peer, aristocrat, nobleman

nobody *pron.* no one/person
n. person of no importance/consequence

noise *n.* din, clamor, tumult, row, clatter, sound, discord, disharmony

none *pron.* no one, nobody, nothing
a. not one, not any

nonsense *n.* silliness, folly, absurdity, foolishness, idiocy, drivel, rubbish

normal *a.* usual, ordinary, regular, customary, habitual, general, standard, accepted, natural

notable *a.* great, famous, renowned, distinguished, noted, eminent, celebrated, illustrious, outstanding, remarkable, momentous, well-known

note *n.* 1. fame, renown, greatness, eminence
2. letter, message, communication
3. jotting, memorandum, record, reminder
4. musical sound
v. observe, notice, acknowledge

notice *v.* see, observe, note, attend, regard
n. 1. warning, advice, announcement, proclamation, bulletin
2. poster, circular, advertisement

notify *v.* inform, advise, tell

notion *n.* idea, fancy, whim, thought, impression, opinion, scheme, plan

nought *n.* nothing, nil, zero

nourish *v.* feed, sustain, care for, succor, nurture, support

novel *a.* new, original, fresh, different, unusual
n. story, tale, work of fiction

novice *n.* learner, beginner, initiate, starter, greenhorn, tyro

nude *a.* naked, bare, without clothes, unclothed, undressed, uncovered, exposed, bald

nudge *v.* push, poke, tap

nuisance *n.* pest, annoyance, offence, injury, bother, trouble, offensive/irritating/vexatious/troublesome/bothersome/annoying person

numb *a.* without feeling/sensation/sensibility, insensate, unfeeling, insensitive, dulled, deadened, paralyzed

number *n.* 1. quantity, amount, sum
2. figure, digit
v. count, total, reckon, compute

numerous *a.* many, a lot of, various, abundant

nutritious *a.* nourishing, wholesome, feeding, strengthening

O o

oaf *n.* lout, dolt, blockhead, fool, idiot, buffoon, clown

oath *n.* 1. solemn promise, pledge, vow
2. swear word, obscenity, profanity, blasphemy

obedient *a.* yielding, submissive, disciplined, dutiful, orderly, law-abiding, observant, compliant

obey *v.* yield/submit to, agree/ comply with, observe

object (ob) *n.* 1. thing, article, item
2. aim, intention, intent, ambition, purpose, hope, goal, target

object (ject) *v.* disapprove, protest, oppose, disagree, argue

obligation *n.* duty, promise, bond, task, responsibility

oblige *v.* 1. help, aid, assist, favor, accommodate
2. make, force, require, expect, compel

obscure a. 1. dark, dim, gloomy, misty, cloudy, hazy, nebulous, overshadowed
2. unknown, little-known, hidden, concealed, doubtful, dubious, indefinite, ambiguous

observant *a.* 1. attentive, watchful, vigilant, alert, careful, cautious
2. obedient, submissive, compliant

observe *v.* 1. look at, regard, notice, see, behold, watch, detect, examine
2. remark, comment, give an opinion
3. obey, submit to, comply with, pay regard to

obstacle *n.* hindrance, handicap, obstruction, bar, barrier, blockage, stoppage, impediment

obstinate *a.* stubborn, obdurate, unyielding, adamant, headstrong, determined, persistent

obstruct *v.* oppose, hinder, handicap, hamper, bar, block, stop, impede, retard

obtain *v.* get, take, secure, procure, acquire, earn, win

obvious *a.* clear, plain, easily seen, unmistakable, apparent, evident

occasion *n.* 1. happening, occurrence, event, incident, episode, affair, circumstance, situation
2. reason, cause, need
v. cause, start, initiate, originate

occasional *a.* infrequent, uncommon, irregular, rare

occupation *n.* 1. work, job, employment, business, trade, profession, vocation, calling, career
2. possession, ownership, residence, tenancy

occupy *v.* take up possession of, live/reside/dwell in, inhabit, possess, own

occur *v.* happen, take place, befall

occurrence *n.* happening, event, affair, incident, episode, experience

odd *a.* 1. strange, unusual, peculiar, queer, abnormal, awkward, absurd, weird, eerie
2. not even, uneven, irregular, not uniform
3. not divisible by two

odious *a.* nasty, unpleasant, distasteful, loathsome, obnoxious, disagreeable, displeasing, repulsive, offensive

odor *n.* smell, scent, perfume, fragrance, aroma

offence *n.* wrong, error, fault, crime, unlawful/illegal act/action, misdemeanor

offend *v.* displease, hurt, harm, sin, insult, snub, vex, anger

offensive *a.* disagreeable, unpleasant, displeasing, nasty, odious, distasteful, obnoxious, objectionable, putrid, foul

offer *v.* proffer, hold out, make available, present, give, volunteer, suggest
n. gift, offering, present, sacrifice

office *n.* 1. study, business headquarters
2. official post/position, duty

officer *n.* commander, leader, official, representative, agent

official *n.* officer, representative, agent
a. authorized, appointed, public

old *a.* 1. olden, ancient, antiquated, old-fashioned, antique, aged, elderly
2. worn, decayed, neglected, unwanted

omit *v.* leave out/undone, exclude, overlook, neglect, evade, disregard, fail, miss

once *adv.* on one/a certain occasion, for/at one time

only *a.* alone, lone, one, sole, single
adv. solely, singly, merely, but, just, exclusively, nothing more
conj. but then, were it not, besides

onward *adv.* onwards, forward, forwards, to the front, in advance

open *a.* 1. unshut, unhidden, uncovered, unclosed
2. sincere, frank, candid
v. 1. unclose, uncover, unfasten, unlock, disclose, reveal, release
2. begin, start, commence
open-eyed: *conscious, watchful, vigilant*
openhanded: *generous, liberal, benevolent*
open-minded: *fair, unbiased, unprejudiced, impartial*

opening *n.* 1. gap,break, hole, aperture, entrance
2. opportunity, chance, occasion
a. starting, beginning, commencing, first, initial

operate *v.* work, act, behave, manage, manipulate, drive

opinion *n.* observation, belief, suggestion, comment

opponent *n.* rival, competitor, antagonist, foe, enemy

opportune *a.* accurately timed, well timed, just right, convenient

opportunity *n.* good chance, opening, occasion

oppose *v.* resist, react, be against, contradict, fight against

opposite *a.* contrary, completely different, facing, face to face, opposed

opposition *n.* 1. antagonism, hostility, hindrance, rivalry, defiance
2. group/party of opponents

oppress *v.* treat harshly/cruelly, overburden, crush, overwhelm, overpower, subjugate, subdue, suppress

opt *v.* pick, prefer, choose, select

optimistic *a.* hopeful, sanguine

option *n.* choice, preference, alternative

oral *a.* verbal, spoken, voiced, unwritten

order *n.* 1. instruction, demand, command, rule, regulation
2. request
3. way, method, technique
4. neatness, tidiness
5. rank, grade, class, category, arrangement, sequence

orderly *a.* 1. ordered, methodical, well arranged/regulated, systematic, neat, tidy
2. well-behaved, well-conducted, disciplined, obedient, not unruly

ordinary *a.* common, commonplace, mediocre, usual, plain, homely, normal, regular, customary, habitual

organization *n.* 1. system, method/way of operating, operation, arrangement
2. business, firm, company, society, establishment

origin *n.* source, beginning, start, cause

originate *v.* invent, devise, begin, start, cause

ornament *n.* decoration, adornment

outbreak *n.* 1. outburst, eruption
2. rebellion, revolt, uprising

outfit *n.* set, collection, apparatus, equipment

outing *n.* trip, excursion, tour, expedition

outlaw *n.* robber, bandit, brigand, desperado, fugitive, renegade, criminal

outlet *n.* way out, egress, exit

outrageous *a.* dreadful, terrible, shocking, inexcusable, atrocious, awful, offensive, obnoxious

outside *adv.* outward, outwards, without
a. external, on the outside

outstanding *a.* superior, excellent, exceptional, famous, celebrated, notable, well-known, prominent

outward *adv.* outwards, outside
a. 1. external, on the outside
2. on the surface, superficial

over *prep.* 1. above, across
2. more than
adv. the opposite/reverse/other (side or face)
a. 1. ended, finished, terminated, closed, completed, done
2. above, upper, covering

overcome *v.* beat, defeat, overpower, vanquish, overthrow, overwhelm, conquer, subdue

overflow *v.* flood, teem, be abundant/plentiful/in excess, proliferate

overlook *v.* 1. pass by/over, ignore, disregard, tolerate, excuse, pardon, forgive
2. supervise, superintend, oversee

overpower *v.* overcome, beat, defeat, vanquish, overthrow, overwhelm, conquer, subdue

overthrow *v.* defeat, bring down, ruin, destroy

overwhelm *v.* defeat, beat, conquer, vanquish, overpower, subdue, overcome, overthrow, swamp

owe *v.* be in debt/a debtor

own *v.* 1. hold, have, possess
2. confess, admit, allow, grant, concede

P p

pace *v.* step, tread, walk, march, stride
n. 1. stride, step
2. speed, velocity, rate

pack *n.* 1. set, stack
2. package, parcel, bundle, case, knapsack, burden, load
3. number, group (of hounds or wolves)
v. press/push/crowd together, compress, cram, fill, load

pad *n.* cushion, stuffing, block, stack
v. 1. stuff, fill
2. tramp, march

pagan *n.* heathen, idolater, barbarian

pain *n.* suffering, distress, anxiety, pang, ache, soreness, poignancy, twinge, agony
take pains: *take trouble/care, make effort*

pair *n.* set of two, couple
v. arrange in couples, join, unite, mate

pale *a.* pallid, white, wan, ashen, grey, pasty, faded, faint, dim

paltry *a.* worthless, trifling, insignificant, petty, contemptible, despicable

pamper *v.* spoil, indulge, pet, coddle, humor

pan *n.* can, tin, dish, bowl, receptacle, container, vessel

pandemonium *n.* disorder, uproar, din, bedlam, tumult, chaos

panic *n.* fear, terror, fright, frenzy, alarm, haste, hurry, excitement, chaos

parade *n.* assembly, march, promenade, procession, display, show, exhibition
v. 1. march, strut
2. muster, assemble

paralyze *v.* make/render powerless/numb, disable, cripple, incapacitate

parched *a.* 1. dry, arid, scorched, shriveled
2. thirsty

pardon *v.* 1. forgive, excuse, overlook, allow, absolve
2. release, set free, discharge, acquit

part *n.* 1. portion, fraction, bit, piece, section, share
2. character, role
v. 1. separate, divide, detach, split
2. take leave

particular *a.* 1. distinct, special, exclusive, individual
2. careful, fastidious, choosy, selective

partner *n.* 1. mate, associate, colleague, companion
2. husband, wife, fiancé, fiancée, friend

party *n.* 1. group, troop, band, faction
2. feast, affair, function, ball, celebration

pass *v.* 1. go/move/travel beyond, exceed
2. transfer, deliver, hand over
3. allow, sanction, approve
n. 1. passage, gap, opening, path
2. ticket, voucher, permit, passport

passage *n.* 1. corridor, alley, lane, route, way, exit, entrance
2. voyage, journey
3. part, section, excerpt

passion *n.* emotion, fervor, devotion, ardor, excitement, fire

paste *n.* gum, glue, adhesive, mucilage, cement, fixative

pastime *n.* sport, recreation, amusement, hobby, pursuit

patch *v.* cover, mend, repair, cobble, sew, darn
n. 1. pad, piece, strip
2. plot, allotment

path *n.* footpath, track, way, route, road, lane

patient *a.* persevering, enduring, uncomplaining, long-suffering, tolerant, calm
n. invalid, sick person

patrol *v.* watch, guard, police, protect

pattern *n.* 1. example, model, sample, specimen
2. design, decoration, figure, arrangement

pause *n.* rest, interval, gap, intermission, recess, stop, halt

pay *v.* 1. discharge, requite, reward, award, remunerate, recompense, compensate
2. suffer, endure
n. payment, wages, salary, earnings

peaceful *a.* quiet, calm, tranquil, serene, restful, placid

peak *n.* 1. highest point, top, tip, crest, crown, summit, pinnacle (of a mountain)
2. brim (of a cap)

peculiar *a.* 1. unusual, uncommon, strange, not normal, odd, eccentric, curious, queer
2. personal, particular

peer *v.* look, glance, stare, peep
n. 1. equal, match
2. nobleman, aristocrat
3. member of the House of Lords

penalty *n.* punishment, fine, imposition

penetrate *v.* enter, pass into/through, pierce, perforate, puncture

pensive *a.* thoughtful, reflective, dreamy, melancholy

people *n.* persons, folk, personnel, individuals

perfect *a.* excellent, faultless, flawless, superb, grand, fine, glorious, ideal, wonderful, exemplary, absolute, entire, complete

perfect *v.* complete, improve

perform *v.* do, act, achieve, accomplish

perfume *n.* scent, fragrance, sweet smell/odor/aroma

perhaps *adv.* maybe, possibly, perchance

peril *n.* danger, jeopardy, risk, hazard, menace, pitfall, trap

perish *v.* 1. die, expire
2. decay, rot, putrefy, decompose, wither, fade

permanent *a.* lasting, enduring, constant, endless, abiding

permit *v.* allow, let, authorize, sanction

permit *n.* pass, passport, license

perpendicular *a.* upright, erect, vertical, straight up

perpetual *a.* ceaseless, unceasing, eternal, everlasting, endless

perplex *v.* baffle, mystify, confound, bewilder, puzzle, confuse

persecute *v.* torment, ill-use, ill-treat, molest, plague, annoy, abuse, oppress, victimize

persevere *v.* strive, persist, try, endeavor

persist *v.* persevere, strive, try, endeavor

person *n.* one, someone, individual, man, woman, human being, mortal

personal *a.* private, privy, own, individual

personnel *n.* employees, staff

persuade *v.* sway, urge, compel, coax, entice, influence, encourage, convince

pest *n.* 1. nuisance. annoyance, plague
2. harmful/destructive animal

pet *n.* favorite, darling, beloved, tamed animal
v. caress, fondle, cuddle, stroke

petty *a.* 1. trivial, unimportant, insignificant, small
2. mean, small-minded, narrow-minded

pick *v.* 1. choose, select, opt, prefer, elect
2. collect, gather, pluck, harvest
n. toothpick, pickaxe

picture *n.* illustration, sketch, drawing, painting, portrait, photograph

piece *n.* part, portion, fraction, bit, fragment, morsel, splinter, chip, lump

pierce *v.* penetrate, pass through/into, enter, stab, punch, perforate, puncture

pile *n.* 1. heap, mound, collection, accumulation, mass, stack
2. post, stake 3 nap, surface (of fabric) *v.* heap, amass, collect, stack, assemble, load

pilot *n.* guide, conductor, steersman, helmsman, navigator, airman, aviator

pinch *v.* nip, squeeze, tweak

pine *v.* 1. yearn, long, crave
2. waste away, fret, languish

pipe *n.* tube, stem, conduit, drain

pit *n.* 1. hole, hollow, cavity, depression, indentation
2. mine, colliery
v. 1. match, set
2. make pits/dents. indent

pitch *v.* 1. hurl, fling, throw, cast, toss
2. move up and down, jolt, jump, shake
3. erect tents, encamp
n. 1. tar, bitumen, asphalt
2. ground, spot, position
3. steepness, inclination

pitiful *a.* pathetic, sorrowful, sad, miserable, wretched, sorry

pity *n.* sympathy, compassion, mercy, consideration, grief, sorrow

place *n.* 1. spot, locality, region, site, position
2. job, employment, office
v. 1. put, position, set, lay, fix, locate, arrange
2. recognize, remember

plague *v.* bother, trouble, disturb, worry, pester, annoy, irritate, vex, tease, torment, tantalize
n. pestilence, epidemic

plain *a.* 1. simple, straightforward, blunt, homely, homespun, unsophisticated, not decorated
2. clear, visible, easily seen/understood, obvious, distinct, unmistakable
3. level, even
n. prairie, steppe, plateau

plan *n.* 1. map, chart, diagram, design
2. scheme, notion, idea, plot, motive, proposal, project, program, course, arrangement

plant *v.* 1. sow, implant, set
2. put, place, position, deposit
n. 1. herb, tree, shrub, weed
2. swindle, frame up, hoax
3. equipment, machinery, factory, mill
plants: *vegetation, plant-life, flora*

play *n.* 1. performance, drama, act, production, theatricals
2. game, sport, amusement, entertainment
v. 1. game, jest, frolic, frisk
2. act, perform

plead *v.* beg, beseech, entreat, implore, pray

pleasant *a.* pleasing, agreeable, delightful, cheerful, likeable, lovely, enjoyable, satisfying

please *v.* gladden, delight, cheer, satisfy, suit, thrill

plentiful *a.* abundant, sufficient, ample, generous, copious

plot *n.* 1. plan, scheme, conspiracy, design
2. thread, theme (of a story or a play)
3. allotment, piece of ground, lot, patch

pluck *v.* gather, pick, snatch, grab, pull/take away, remove, harvest
n. bravery, courage, daring, spirit

plump *a.* fat, stout, chubby, obese, rotund

plunder *v.* ravage, sack, despoil, maraud, loot, rob, steal
n. loot, spoil, stolen goods

plunge *v.* 1. dive, dip, immerse, submerge
2. thrust, push, force, drive

point *n.* 1. tip, end
2. aim, purpose, object
3. place, position, location
4. headland, bluff, cape
v. aim, direct, level, line up

poke *v.* prod, jab, push, thrust, nudge

polish *v.* make smooth/shiny/glossy/lustrous, buff, burnish, rub
n. 1. brightness, gloss, shine
2. courtesy, politeness, refinement

polite *a.* courteous, civil, well-mannered, mannerly, refined, gracious

poor *a.* 1. impoverished, needy, in want/poverty, destitute
2. barren, infertile
3. inferior, mediocre, indifferent, miserable

popular *a.* favorite, well-liked

population *n.* people, inhabitants, citizens

portable *a.* movable, transportable, mobile

portion *n.* part, fraction, section, bit, piece, fragment, segment, share

position *n.* 1. place, location, spot, site, point
2. job, employment, situation, office, rank, post, status, station
3. posture, attitude

positive *a.* certain, sure, definite, confident, assured, absolute

possess *v.* own, hold, have, keep, occupy

possibly *adv.* perhaps, maybe, perchance

post *n.* 1. job, employment, situation, position, office, station
2. place, location, spot
3. stake, pole, beam, upright, support
4. mail, letters, correspondence

poster *n.* notice, placard, display, advertisement, bill

postpone *v.* put/carry forward, put off, defer, delay

pot *n.* jar, vessel, container, pan, bowl, dish, basin
v. plant/preserve in pots

poverty *n.* need, want, shortage, impoverishment, scarcity, destitution

power *n.* 1. ability, action, influence, control, mastery, authority
2. effort, strength, might, energy, force, vigor

practicable *a.* workable, usable, useful, operational, effective

practical *a.* skilled, skilful, efficient

practice *n.* 1. exercise, drill, training
2. habit, custom, manner, method, procedure

praise *v.* 1. applaud, commend, speak well of, approve, compliment
2. worship, extol, glorify

preceding *a.* previous, prior, former, earlier, recent, preliminary, preparatory

precious *a.* costly, expensive, valuable, priceless, prized, treasured, cherished, much-loved, esteemed, admired

precise *a.* exact, accurate, fine, concise, specific, correct

predicament *n.* difficulty, plight, dilemma,

prefer *v.* 1. like/want/desire/fancy more, choose, pick, select, favor
2. promote

prejudice *n.* bias, partiality, unfairness, intolerance

preliminary *a.* introductory, opening, preparatory, preceding

prepare *v.* arrange, plan, organize, provide, take precautions, make/get ready

preposterous *a.* ridiculous, absurd, mad, nonsensical, silly, crazy, stupid, foolish, fantastic

presence *n.* attendance, existence, appearance

present *a.* here, existing, in person
n. gift, offer, donation, award
at present: *now, nowadays at this time/the moment*

present *v.* 1. bestow, donate, give, offer
2. introduce, announce, display, exhibit

presently *adv.* shortly, soon, before long, directly

preserve *n.* 1. jam, jelly, confection, pickles, conserve
2. sanctuary
v. protect, guard, maintain, shelter, keep safe, conserve

press *v.* 1. push, squeeze, crush, compress, embrace
2. iron, smooth
3. urge, compel, drive, persuade, encourage
n. 1. printing machine/press, journalism
2. mob, crowd
press on: *hurry, hasten, rush, dash*

pressing *a.* urgent, demanding, immediate, important

pressure *n.* force, effort, power, strength, stress, strain, tension

presume *v.* 1. suppose, assume, take for granted, conclude, believe
2. take the liberty to/of

pretty *a.* pleasing, nice, delicate, dainty, attractive, handsome, beautiful, lovely

prevent *v.* avoid, preclude, stop, check, halt, arrest, prohibit, hinder, obstruct

previous *a.* preceding, prior, former, earlier, recent

price *n.* cost, charge, value, rate, expense

priceless *a.* very valuable/costly/expensive, invaluable, beyond price, precious, irreplaceable

prime *a.* 1. first, primary, chief, main, principal
2. first-rate, perfect, superb, excellent, splendid
n. beginning/earlier part/dawn of life, youth, fullness of health, vigor

principal *a.* chief, main, head, leading, foremost, most important
n. chief, leader, head, director

principle *n.* rule, law, regulation, belief, truth, conviction

prison *n.* jail, penitentiary, reformatory, cell, dungeon

prisoner *n.* captive, convict, accused

private *a.* 1. personal, privy, individual
2. secret, confidential
3. remote, isolated, secluded

prize *v.* 1. value, esteem, treasure, cherish
2. force/pry (open/apart)
n. reward, gift, award, trophy, honor

probable *a.* likely, possible, almost/nearly certain/sure

problem *n.* 1. puzzle, riddle, question, exercise
2. difficulty, burden, worry, trouble, hindrance

procedure *n.* method, way, process, plan, technique, arrangement, approach, action, movement

proceed *v.* 1. begin, commence, start
2. move/travel forward, advance, continue
3. act, behave

proclaim *v.* announce, declare, publish

produce *v.* 1. create, make, manufacture
2. yield, give, bring forth

product *n.* 1. produce, goods, item, article
2. result, consequence

profession *n.* 1. job, employment, trade, business, occupation, calling, vocation, career
2. declaration, admission, proclamation

profit *n.* gain, return, proceeds, benefit, advantage

program *n.* list, plan, scheme, schedule, catalog

progress *v.* move/travel forward, advance, continue, proceed, improve, grow, develop

prohibit *v.* forbid, disallow, ban, bar, stop, deny, prevent

project *n.* plan, scheme, design, task, undertaking, ventur

project *v.* 1. stick/jut out, protrude, extend
2. throw, thrust, fling, hurl, shoot, eject

prolong *v.* lengthen, make longer, extend, increase, expand, stretch, continue

prominent *a.* 1. famous, celebrated, notable, eminent, well-known
2. outstanding, clearly/plainly seen

promise *n.* intention, assurance, guarantee, pledge, agreement, vow

promising *a.* encouraging, hopeful, optimistic

prompt *a.* immediate, without delay, quick, fast, rapid, speedy, swift, ready, punctual
v. encourage, help, assist, inspire

pronounce *v.* utter, articulate, speak distinctly/clearly

propel *v.* push/send/force forward, thrust, drive, impel

proper *a.* correct, just, right, exact, appropriate, suitable, becoming, fitting, seemly, demure

property *n.* 1. possessions, belongings, land, wealth, assets
2. characteristic, quality, nature

propose *v.* offer, suggest, submit, recommend, put forward

prosper *v.* succeed, thrive, grow, flourish, do well, become wealthy

protect *v.* shield, shelter, defend, guard, keep safe, preserve

protest *v.* object, oppose, grumble, complain, disagree

proud *a.* 1. vain, conceited, disdainful, haughty, boastful, self-satisfied, arrogant
2. dignified, stately, noble

prove *v.* 1. find proof/evidence of/for, confirm, verify, demonstrate, show
2. check, test, examine

proverb *n.* maxim, adage, saying, byword

provide *v.* supply, give, furnish, arrange, prepare, equip, provision, produce

provisions *n.* supplies, foodstuffs, victuals

prowl *v.* steal about, lurk, roam, wander

prudent *a.* wise, sagacious, careful, cautious, thrifty, wary, far seeing, far sighted

public *n.* people, populace, inhabitants, community, society

publish *v.* make known, reveal, announce, proclaim, broadcast

pull *v.* draw, tug, tow, yank, snatch, haul, drag, attract

punch *v.* 1. strike, thump, poke, pummel, hit
2. pierce, perforate, puncture

punish *v.* chastise, correct, discipline, penalize, take revenge

pupil *n.* learner, scholar, student

purchase *v.* buy, acquire, gain

pure *a.* 1. clean, unadulterated, unmixed, untainted, spotless, immaculate, genuine
2. innocent, blameless, chaste, stainless, unblemished, perfect, unsullied, virtuous

purify *v.* 1. make pure, clean, cleanse, refine, filter
2. free from sin, absolve

purpose *n.* meaning, intention, object, aim, plan, ambition

pursue *v.* hunt, chase, follow, seek, track

push *v.* thrust, shove, press, prod, poke, nudge

puzzle *n.* problem, riddle, poser, maze
v. perplex, baffle, mystify, bewilder, confuse, confound

Q q

quack *n.* 1. duck's cry, harsh voice, discordant sound
2. humbug, impostor, charlatan, mountebank, pretender, deceiver
v. talk loudly and foolishly, speak boastfully
quack doctor: *vendor/ prescriber of inferior medicines/remedies*

quagmire *n.* bog, marsh, morass, mire, swamp, slough, fen

quake *v.* shake, shiver, tremble, shudder, quiver, quaver, rock, vibrate, throb

qualified *a.* trained, able, competent, capable, experienced, fit, suitable

qualify *v.* 1. train, prepare, make competent/capable/fit/ suitable, give/obtain qualification/diploma/ certificate/degree
2. modify, make limitations/reservations, moderate, mitigate, alter, improve, change, make less absolute, amend

quality *n.* 1. kind, character, grade, standard, class, group, category, degree, badness/goodness of
2. characteristic, attribute, trait, faculty, accomplishment, skill, talent

qualm *n.* 1. doubt, uneasiness, disquiet, misgiving, conscience, scruple
2. momentary/touch of faintness/sickness/nausea

quantity *n.* amount, number, size, measure, mass, weight, volume, estimate, sum, total, part, portion, proportion, extent

quarrel *v.* dispute/differ/disagree/ argue/contend angrily, wrangle, altercate, squabble, row, fall out, bicker, find fault, take exception

quarry *n.* hunted/pursued/chased animal/person, prey, game, intended victim

quarters *n.* accommodation, lodgings, abode, residence, billet, barracks, cabin

quash *v.* crush, subdue, suppress, quell, annul, make void, invalidate, put/make an end to, terminate, ban, bar, disallow, oppose, reject

queer *a.* 1. peculiar, odd, strange, not ordinary/normal, abnormal, unusual, bizarre, eccentric, suspect, suspicious, shady, questionable, doubtful, dubious
2. out of sorts, unwell, ill, sick, indisposed, giddy, faint, drunk

quell *v.* crush, subdue, suppress, overcome, put down, force to/make submit

quench *v.* 1. extinguish, put out, destroy
2. end, satisfy, slake (thirst), cool (with water)

query *v.* question, inquire, check, investigate

quest *n.* search, inquiry, hunt, chase, pursuit, investigation

question *v.* ask questions about, query, inquire, seek information from, interrogate, examine, oppose, raise objection to, doubt, be dubious about, dispute

questionable *a.* doubtful, in doubt, dubious, debatable, disputable, in dispute, unsure, uncertain, possibly untrue, not consistent, inconsistent

quick *a.*
1. quick-moving, rapid, fast, speedy, swift, fleet, brisk, sudden, immediate, instantaneous
2. agile, nimble, spry, active, lively, alive, energetic, vigorous, alert, quick-witted, keen, eager
3. sharp, short, snappy, abrupt, curt, brusque, hasty, impatient, impetuous, harsh, irritable, irascible

quiet *a.*
1. silent, without noise, noiseless, subdued, hushed, inaudible
2. still, restful, at rest, tranquil, peaceful, serene, demure, reposed, undisturbed, docile, placid, unmotivated, inactive, unobtrusive

She wore a **quiet** dress.

quit *v.*
1. leave, go away/depart/ retire from, go out of, vacate, desert
2. forsake, let go, give up, resign, abandon, relinquish, surrender
3. stop, cease, discontinue

quitter: *deserter, coward, poltroon, shirker, slacker*

quite *adv.*
1. completely, entirely, fully, wholly, altogether, to the fullest/utmost extent, positively, definitely, absolutely, truly, really
2. rather, to some extent, fairly, more or less

quiver *v.* tremble, shake, shiver, shudder, quake, quaver, twitch, vibrate, throb, rock

n. sheath, holder, case, container

The archer keeps his arrows in a **quiver.**

quiz *n.* set of questions/queries/ problems/puzzles/riddles, questionnaire, test, examination, interrogation

quotation *n.*
1. words/passage quoted, exact copy/repeat of the words, quote, extract, excerpt, selection
2. price quoted/given/ named/stated

R r

race *v.* flow, run, sprint, dash, hurry, hasten, speed
n. 1. flow, current, stream
2. contest, competition, match
3. family, tribe, clan, stock people, nation

rack *n.* frame, framework, shelves
v. pain, hurt, torment, torture, agonize

racket *n.* 1. uproar, din, row, noise, bedlam, disturbance, tumult, hubbub, commotion
2. bat, racquet
3. fraud, swindle

radiate *v.* scatter, spread, shed, broadcast, give/send off/out, transmit, emit

rage *n.* anger, annoyance, fury, frenzy, wrath, passion

ragged *a.* torn, tattered, threadbare, shabby

raid *v.* attack, invade, plunder, loot, pillage, ravage

rail *n.* beam, bar, barrier, fence
v. scold, threaten, abuse

raise *v.* 1. erect, elevate, lift, hoist
2. increase, advance
3. grow, cultivate, rear, breed
4. bring up, educate
5. collect, gather, levy (taxes, soldiers, etc.)
6. stir up, agitate, rouse
raise Cain: *stir up trouble, make a fuss/disturbance*

ramble *v.* 1. stroll, roam, wander, straggle, walk
2. digress, wander away, stray from the subject

range *n.* 1. extent, scope, limit, spread
2. line, row, rank
v. roam, rove, wander, stroll, straggle

rank *n.* 1. line, row, range, queue
2. class, category, quality, grade, order, position, status
a. 1. luxuriant, coarse, gross, choked
2. rotting, decaying, foul-smelling, indecent, corrupt
3. unmistakable, flagrant, virulent

ransack *v.* search thoroughly, loot, plunder, pillage, sack

rap *n.* 1. tap, knock, bump, thump, whack, slap, blow, bang
2. jot, bit, little/least bit

rapid *a.* quick, fast, swift, speedy

rare *a.* uncommon, unusual, scarce, infrequent, extraordinary, peculiar, odd

rascal *n.* rogue, scamp, imp, vagabond, scoundrel, ruffian, villain, culprit

rash *a.* reckless, wild, headstrong, impetuous, foolhardy, hasty, careless, thoughtless

rate *n.* 1. price, cost, charge, value, amount
2. estimate, assessment, appraisal
3. velocity, speed, swiftness, pace

rather *adv.* 1. sooner, preferably, more truly, for choice
2. to some extent, slightly, somewhat

rattle *n.* noise, sound, din, clatter, chatter, babble
v. confuse, fluster, frighten, make nervous/apprehensive

rave *v.* 1. shout/yell/talk wildly/madly/furiously, rage, roar, rant, fume
2. be excited/thrilled, enthuse

ravenous *a.* very hungry/greedy, starving, famished, voracious

raw *a.* 1. fresh, uncooked, unprepared
2. untrained, inexperienced
3. sore, sensitive
4. very cold, bitter, bleak, chilly

ready *a.* 1. willing, prepared, available, handy
2. prompt, quick, speedy, swift, immediate

real *a.* actual, authentic, true, genuine, honest

realize *v.* 1. understand, comprehend, appreciate, recognize, know, be aware
2. make realistic
3. convert, amass, fetch
The sale **realized** $146.95.

rear *a.* back, hindmost, rearmost
n. end, back, background
v. 1. bring up, train, educate
2. raise, breed
3. build, erect, raise lip

reason *n.* 1. cause, purpose, motive,
2. aim mind, intelligence, intellect, judgement
v. think, judge, conclude

reasonable *a.* proper, right, just, sensible, fair, moderate

rebel *v.* revolt, mutiny, disobey

rebel *n.* revolutionary, traitor, insurgent, mutineer

recall *v.* 1. remember, recollect
2. call/summon back
3. take/bring back, withdraw

receive *v.* take, accept, gain, obtain, acquire, get

recent *a.* 1. latest, new, modern
2. preceding, foregoing, previous

recite *v.* repeat, relate, retell, narrate, deliver, quote

reckless *a.* rash, wild, headstrong, impetuous, foolhardy, hasty, careless, thoughtless, harum-scarum

reckon *v.* count, calculate, estimate, judge, compute

recline *v.* rest, repose, lie, loll, lean back, sprawl

recognize *v.* 1. remember, recollect, recall, know, identify
2. admit, accept, comprehend, understand, appreciate, see, know, realize

recollect *v.* recall, remember, call to mind

recommend *v.* advise, suggest, commend, approve of, make acceptable

record *n.* 1. written account, note, list, inventory, report, memorandum, entry
2. best/finest achievement/result
3. disc, tape, cassette

recover *v.* 1. get/bring/fetch/win back, regain, restore, reclaim
2. become/get well/better, return/restore to health, improve, revive, recuperate

recreation *n.* leisure, amusement, game, sport, pursuit, hobby, interest, pastime

reduce *v.* 1. lessen, decrease, shrink, contract, diminish, bring down
2. convert, change
3. conquer, subdue
4. weaken, impoverish

reflect *v.* 1. consider, think over, meditate, ponder, study
2. rebound, return, mirror, reproduce

reform *v.* 1. rearrange, change, alter
2. improve, better, correct, amend

refresh *v.* freshen, renew, enliven, restore, revive, strengthen, stimulate

refuge *n.* place of safety, shelter, sanctuary, haven, retreat, protection

refuse *v.* decline, reject, turn down, put aside

refuse *n.* rubbish, waste, litter, garbage

regain *v.* get/bring/fetch/win back, recover, retrieve

regard *v.* look at, observe, view, behold
n. esteem, admiration, approval

region *n.* area, section, part, locality, district, territory, land, country

register *n.* record, official list, roll, inventory

regret *v.* be sorry, bewail, repent, apologize, mourn, grieve, lament

regular *a.* 1. constant, permanent
2. correct, proper, normal, customary, usual, standard
3. methodical

rehearse *v.* perfect, practice, repeat

reject *v.* refuse, decline, return, discard, throw out, eliminate

relate *v.* 1. tell, say, state, narrate, recount, describe
2. belong, connect, associate

relax *v.* 1. abate, become less severe/powerful, reduce, lessen, release, slacken
2. take ease/comfort, rest

release *v.* free, liberate, set free/loose, relax, discharge, let go, unfasten

reliable *a.* dependable, trustworthy, loyal, faithful, sure, safe, certain, accurate

relieve *v.* 1. help, assist, aid, soothe, ease, alleviate, palliate, comfort
2. take over from, replace

reluctant *a.* unwilling, not willing/keen/anxious, loath, hesitant

rely *v.* depend, trust, count

remain *v.* 1. stay, rest, linger, loiter, tarry
2. survive, endure, last

remark *v.* 1. say, comment, mention
2. observe, notice, note

remarkable *a.* unusual, uncommon, noteworthy, amazing, extraordinary, marvelous, wonderful

remedy *v.* cure, heal, restore, repair, relieve
n. cure, restorative, prescription, treatment

remember *v.* 1. recall, recollect, bring to mind
2. think of/about, mention
3. reward, tip

remind *v.* prompt, jog memory

remote *a.* distant, far off/away, isolated, lonely, secluded

remove *v.* 1. take from/away, sequester, displace, detach
2. transfer, convey, carry
3. dismiss, sack

repair *v.* 1. remedy, restore, mend, patch, cobble, overhaul, correct
2. go, depart, travel

repay *v.* reward, pay back, return, refund

repeat *v.* say/do again, copy, reproduce, retell, recite, recount

replace *v.* 1. put back, return, restore
2. substitute, exchange

reply *v.* answer, retort, respond, echo

report *n.* 1. statement, account, comment, message, story, rumor, news, advice, intelligence, declaration, announcement, disclosure
2. explosion, bang, noise

reproduce *v.* 1. repeat, copy, duplicate, print, trace
2. breed, multiply

require *v.* 1. want, need, desire, wish for
2. ask, request, solicit

rescue *v.* aid, help, free/remove/deliver from danger, save, recover

research *n.* study, inquiry, investigation

reserve *v.* store, keep, retain, save, withhold, set aside, book, arrange

reserved *a.* 1. booked, saved, kept, set aside, retained
2. shy, modest, quiet, bashful, retiring

reside *v.* live, dwell, abide, lodge, inhabit, occupy

residence *n.* dwelling, home, house, quarters

resign *v.* leave, quit, give up, surrender, retire

resist *v.* withstand, oppose, defy, check, thwart

resolution *n.* 1. resolve, intention, aim, decision, plan, scheme
2. determination, strength of purpose

resourceful *a.* ingenious, skilful, inventive, imaginative

respect *n.* esteem, appreciation, honor, regard, admiration

respectable *a.* worthy, honorable, decent, proper

responsible *a.* 1. answerable, liable, accountable
2. dependable, reliable, trustworthy

restful *a.* relaxing, comfortable, easy, leisurely, quiet, placid, peaceful, tranquil, soothing

restless *a.* uneasy, unsettled, agitated, fidgety, disturbed, apprehensive

restore *v.* 1. replace, return, give/put/pay/bring back, refund, repay
2. repair, mend
3. heal, cure, revive, make well

restrain *v.* check, hold back, stop, hinder, restrict, control, prevent

restrict *v.* limit, confine, restrain, control, hold back

result *n.* answer, outcome, effect, consequence, product, conclusion

resume *v.* begin/commence/start again, go on, continue, proceed with

retire *v.* withdraw, retreat, depart, go away/back

retort *n.* reply, response, answer

return *v.* 1. put/give/bring back, restore, recover, replace
2. come/go/travel back, reappear
n. 1. restoration, recovery
2. reappearance
3. repayment, refund
4. profit, gain, proceeds

reveal *v.* disclose, unveil, unmask, expose, show

reverse *v.* 1. turn round/inside out
2. go/move/travel backwards
3. cancel, undo, alter
n. 1. opposite/other
2. defeat, failure, loss

revise *v.* correct, alter, change, improve, amend

revive *v.* refresh, restore, renew

revolt *v.* rebel, disobey, mutiny, desert
n. rebellion, mutiny, desertion

revolting *a.* horrible, hideous, disgusting, loathsome, offensive, very unpleasant, noxious, odious, repulsive

revolve *v.* turn, spin, rotate, whirl, gyrate

reward *n.* payment, gift, prize, profit, bonus

ribald *a.* obscene, irreverent, scurrilous

rich *a.* 1. wealthy, prosperous
2. abundant, rank, luxuriant, fertile, fruitful
3. bright, gaudy, deep, vivid

riddle *n.* problem, puzzle, secret, mystery
v. perforate, puncture

ridicule *v.* mock, make fun of, laugh/jeer at, tease
n. scorn, sarcasm, mockery, jeers

ridiculous *a.* absurd, silly, nonsensical, foolish, stupid, unreasonable, preposterous

right *a.* correct, proper, just, true, fair, exact, appropriate, suitable, lawful
n. liberty, privilege

rigid *a.* stiff, firm, unbending

ring *n.* circle, circlet, loop, band, enclosure
v. sound, tinkle, jingle, chime

ripe *a.* full-grown, mature, ready, mellow, fully developed

rise *v.* 1. arise, get/stand up
2. ascend, climb, go upwards
3. increase, swell, expand
4. originate, begin
n. hill, mound, slope, elevation

risk *n.* danger, peril, hazard, chance, dare

rival *n.* opponent, competitor, adversary, enemy

road *n.* highway, route, track, path, way, thoroughfare

roam *v.* wander, ramble, stroll, walk, stray, straggle

rob *v.* steal, loot, plunder, maraud, pillage, raid, pilfer

robber *n.* bandit, brigand, ruffian, raider, pirate, footpad, highwayman, thief, burglar

robust *a.* strong, healthy, sturdy, hardy, vigorous, virile

rock *v.* sway, stagger, reel, wobble
n. stone, pebble, boulder

rogue *n.* rascal, vagabond, scoundrel, ruffian, scapegrace, scamp, imp, villain

roll *v.* 1. turn over, rotate, revolve, wind, reel, spin
2. flatten, level, press
n. 1. register, official list, catalog, inventory
2. bun, small loaf

romantic *a.* fanciful, imaginative, sentimental

root *n.* 1. foundation, bottom, base
2. cause, reason, origin, beginning, source

rot *v.* decay, perish, putrefy, decompose, spoil

rotate *v.* turn, spin, revolve, roll, whirl

rough *a.* 1. coarse, uneven, irregular
2. wild, stormy, disorderly
3. severe, harsh
4. uncouth, boorish, common, vulgar, rude, crude

round *a.* 1. ball-shaped, spherical, globular
2. circle-shaped, ring-shaped, circular, smooth

rouse *v.* arouse, awaken, wake, wake up, stir up, alarm, startle, stimulate

rout *v.* defeat, beat, vanquish, conquer, put to flight

route *n.* way, course, road, path, track

routine *a.* orderly, systematic, customary, regular, general, usual

row *n.* 1. quarrel, dispute, disagreement, altercation
2. noise, din, clatter, bedlam, uproar, tumult, disturbance, commotion

rub *v.* 1. stroke, massage
2. smear, wipe, scratch, mark

rubbish *n.* waste, litter, junk, trash, debris, refuse, garbage, lumber

rude *a.* coarse, common, vulgar, boorish, uncouth, impolite, discourteous, rough

ruin *v.* wreck, destroy, spoil, damage

rumor *n.* news, gossip, hearsay, tattle, talk, tale

run *v.* 1. move/travel fast/quickly/swiftly, flow, race, career, sprint, spurt, dash, glide, dart, scamper, speed, rush
2. manage, direct, control
n. trip, journey, excursion

rural *a.* country, rustic, of the countryside, agricultural

rush *v.* move/travel quickly/swiftly, dash, stampede, charge, career, hasten, hurry, speed

ruthless *a.* without pity/mercy, harsh, pitiless, merciless, cruel, brutal

S s

sack *v.* 1. dismiss (from job/employment), fire
2. plunder, pillage, loot, ravage
n. large bag

sacred *a.* holy, consecrated, sanctified, hallowed, dedicated, sacrosanct, revered

sad *a.* unhappy, sorrowful, miserable, gloomy, dejected, downcast, depressed, dismal, woeful, melancholy, doleful, mournful, lugubrious

safe *a.* 1. secure, protected, sheltered
2. trustworthy, reliable, dependable

sample *n.* specimen, example, pattern, model, illustration
v. take/give samples, try, test

satisfactory *a.* suitable, adequate, acceptable, appropriate

satisfy *v.* please, content, suit, gratify

saturated *a.* soaked, drenched, sodden, soggy

saucy *a.* cheeky, impertinent, impudent, forward, bold, brazen, rude, flippant

savage *a.* 1. wild, untamed, fierce, ferocious
2. barbarous, uncivilized, cruel, brutal
3. angry, enraged, furious, mad, violent

save *v.* 1. rescue, deliver, liberate, set free
2. safeguard, store, keep, gather, hoard, put by, preserve, collect
3. economize, be sparing/careful/thrifty
prep. except, leaving out, omitting

say *v.* state, speak, utter, tell, declare, announce, express, assert

saying *n.* proverb, byword, maxim, adage

scamp *n.* rascal, scapegrace, rogue, imp, scallywag, scoundrel knave
v. skimp, dodge

scanty *a.* meager, skimpy, sparse, inadequate, insufficient, little, poor

scarce *a.* meager, rare, short, sparse, not plentiful, insufficient

scare *v.* frighten, alarm, startle, terrify

scatter *v.* 1. strew, sprinkle, spread, sow, broadcast, distribute
2. separate, disperse, break up

scene *n.* view, vista, sight, landscape, panorama

scent *n.* smell, odor, perfume, fragrance, aroma

scheme *n.* plan, design, plot, project, undertaking, venture

scoff *v.* mock, jeer, sneer, deride, gibe (jibe), taunt, ridicule

scold *v.* rebuke, reprimand, reprove, criticize, find fault with

scorn *v.* despise, spurn, disdain, be contemptuous, sneer, reject, condemn

scoundrel *n.* rogue, rascal, villain, scamp, scallywag, knave

scrap *n.* 1. bit, piece, portion, remnant, morsel, shred, fragment
2. waste, rubbish, junk, refuse
v. 1. discard, throw away
2. quarrel, fight, brawl

scratch *v.* tear, claw, mark, disfigure

scrawl *v.* scribble, write hastily/badly

scream *v.* cry/shout loudly, bawl, yell, shriek, screech, squeal, bellow

screen *n.* 1. cover, protection, shelter, mask
2. partition, divider
3. sieve, net

search *v.* look for, seek, explore, probe, ransack

secret *a.* hidden, concealed, unknown, confidential, mysterious

section *n.* part, portion, fraction, piece, segment, sector, division, region

secure *a.* safe, fast, tight, firm, solid, stable
v. 1. obtain, get, procure
2. fortify, make safe, enclose
3. fasten, tie up, moor

see *v.* 1. look at, observe, perceive, regard, watch
2. know, understand, comprehend, follow, grasp

seize *v.* 1. grab, grip, grasp, clutch, hold
2. capture, arrest, take
3. steal, rob, snatch, plunder, loot, carry off, annex

seldom *adv.* not often, rarely, infrequently, occasionally

select *v.* pick, choose, designate, indicate

sell *v.* vend, deal/trade in, market, retail, peddle

send *v.* dispatch, forward, transmit, propel, drive

senseless *a.* 1. without sense, stupid, silly, foolish, nonsensical, ridiculous, pointless, absurd
2. insensible, unconscious

sensible *a.* 1. intelligent, not foolish, wise, thoughtful, practical, astute, shrewd
2. conscious, aware, alert

separate *a.* divided, disconnected, distinct, unconnected, detached, apart, individual

serene *a.* calm, tranquil, composed, untroubled, undisturbed, peaceful, placid

serious *a.* 1. grave, critical
2. solemn, sober, sombre, dignified, important
3. thoughtful, pensive, earnest, sincere

set *v.* 1. place, put, plant, stand, sink
2. harden, solidify, become hard/solid
n. group, pack, kit, outfit

settle *v.* 1. rest, alight, sink
2. pay
3. arrange, determine, decide
settle in: *colonize, inhabit*

sever *v.* cut, separate, divide

severe *a.* 1. stern, strict, harsh, stiff
2. plain, simple, austere, unadorned
3. intense, violent

shabby *a.* 1. threadbare, worn, poor, drab, ragged, dilapidated
2. paltry, petty, mean, miserable, spiteful, unfair, unkind

shady *a.* 1. shaded, shadowy, darkened, gloomy
2. dishonest, crooked, suspicious

shake *v.* 1. tremble, shiver, quake, quiver, shudder, wobble, vibrate, agitate
2. wave, brandish, flourish

sham *a.* false, bogus, feigned, pretended, imitation, counterfeit

shame *v.* disgrace, dishonor, discredit, humiliate

shameless *a.* without shame, bold, brazen, forward, rude, vulgar, common, indecent, disgraceful

shape *v.* form, fashion, mold, construct, build
n. form, figure, outline, pattern, contour

share *v.* 1. divide, allot, apportion, ration
2. take part, participate

sharp *a.* 1. keen, pointed, piercing, penetrating, cutting
2. painful, stinging, bitter, pungent, biting, acid, severe, harsh
3. quick-witted, alert, bright, smart, intelligent, clever, shrewd, astute, vigilant, wary, watchful

sheer *a.* 1. abrupt, steep
2. complete, absolute, utter
3. transparent, thin

shelter *n.* shield, screen, protection, cover, refuge, harbor, sanctuary, haven

shield *n.* shelter, screen, cover, protection, guard

shift *v.* 1. move/change/alter position
2. manage, make do, carry on, survive, exist

shine *v.* give out/emit/radiate light, glow, glisten, gleam
n. brightness, luster, brilliance, gloss

shiver *v.* shake, tremble, quake, quiver, shudder

shock *n.* 1. fright, alarm
2. blow, collision, impact, jolt, shake
v. startle, frighten, alarm, dismay, appall, astound, astonish

short *a.* 1. not long/lengthy/tall, small, brief, concise, laconic
2. scanty, meager, lacking, insufficient, deficient, in need
3. curt, terse, abrupt, sharp, quick, nasty, uncivil

shortage *n.* lack, inadequacy, insufficiency, deficiency

shout *v.* cry/call loudly, yell, bawl, bellow, scream

show *v.* 1. display, reveal, exhibit, demonstrate, present
2. explain, guide, instruct

shred *n.* scrap, fragment, bit, piece, flake, shaving, strip
v. tear, rip, fragment

shrewd *a.* wise, sagacious, discerning, astute, knowing, observant, alert, sharp, clever, cunning

shrill *a.* keen, piercing, penetrating, high-pitched, loud, sharp

shut *a.* 1. not open, closed, fastened
2. confined, enclosed, contained

shy *a.* timid, cautious, wary, reserved, reticent, modest, bashful
v. throw, toss, pitch, hurl
shy away: *hang back, take fright*

sick *a.* ill, unwell, ailing, indisposed, unhealthy

sign *n.* signal, token, symbol, trace, mark, emblem, badge, indication, gesture

signal *v.* beckon, gesture, indicate, betoken, send a message
n. sign, symbol
a. noteworthy, worthwhile, memorable

significant *a.* important, notable, noteworthy, meaningful, prominent, expressive

silent *a.* quiet, without noise/sound, noiseless, soundless, still, hushed

silly *a.* foolish, stupid, absurd, daft, senseless, nonsensical, puerile, pointless, ridiculous, inane, simple-minded, simple-witted

simple *a.* 1. not difficult, easy, elementary
2. plain, unadorned, austere
3. open, frank, candid, honest, straightforward, true, truthful

sincere *a.* honest, true, genuine, straightforward, not hypocritical, trustworthy

site *n.* location, situation, place, spot, position, ground

situation *n.* 1. site, location, place, spot
2. position, appointment, job, employment, office
3. predicament, plight

skillful *a.* skilled, able, expert, clever, capable, competent, efficient, dexterous

slack *a.* 1. loose, limp, flabby, flaccid
2. lazy, slow, indolent, lax, negligent, indifferent, careless

slay *v.* kill, slaughter, massacre, destroy

sleek *a.* smooth, glossy, shiny, velvety, silky, lustrous

sleep *v.* slumber, repose, doze

slender *a.* 1. slim, thin, narrow
2. slight, scanty, meager, insufficient, inadequate

slight *a.* 1. small, trifling, trivial, insignificant, unimportant
2. slim, slender, thin, delicate
v. insult, ignore, disregard, neglect, snub

slim *a.* 1. slender, thin, narrow
2. delicate, fragile, slight, frail, weak

slip *n.* 1. stumble, stagger, fall
2. mistake, error, fault, blunder
3. small piece/sheet of paper, note

sly *a.* crafty, cunning, artful, deceitful, underhanded, treacherous, stealthy

small *a.* little, tiny, slight, undersized, puny, paltry, insignificant, trivial, unimportant, trifling

smart *a.* 1. clever, talented, bright, intelligent, sharp, alert, keen, shrewd
2. neat, tidy, handsome, stylish, fashionable
3. sharp, biting, stinging

smell *n.* scent, odor, fragrance, aroma, perfume, stink, stench

smooth *a.* 1. even, flat, level, polished
2. calm, peaceful, tranquil, still, serene, placid

snatch *v.* grab, grip, seize, grasp, take, clutch

sneer *v.* scorn, disdain, taunt, jeer, gibe (jibe), mock, belittle

sob *v.* cry, weep, gulp

sober *a.* calm, sensible, grave, dignified, demure, temperate, not drunk/inebriated/intoxicated

soft *a.* 1. not hard/solid, yielding, weak, limp, pliable, flexible
2. gentle, tender, mild, kind, sympathetic
3. low, subdued

soggy *a.* saturated, soaked, drenched, sodden, wet, damp, moist

solemn *a.* serious, grave, sober, sad, sorrowful, mournful, dignified

solid *a.* 1. not hollow/empty, firm, hard, rigid
2. sound, reliable, wise, dependable, stable, steady, steadfast, trustworthy, sensible

solitary *a.* 1. lone, alone, single, only, sole
2. lonely, desolate, barren, deserted, isolated, secluded, remote

soothe *v.* smooth, ease, placate, quiet, calm, alleviate, relieve, comfort, soften

sore *a.* 1. painful, hurting, raw, tender, irritated, smarting, aching
2. offended, vexed, cross

sorrow *n.* sadness, unhappiness, misery, grief, woe, suffering, distress, remorse, anxiety, heartache

sorry *a.* 1. sorrowful, sad, grieved, regretful, remorseful, penitent
2. poor, miserable, unfortunate, wretched, pathetic, pitiful

sort *n.* kind, type, group, grade, class, quality, nature

sound *n.* 1. noise, din, clamor
2. channel, strait
a. 1. wise, sensible, correct, right, reliable, intelligent, good
2. whole, complete, strong, healthy, hearty, sturdy, vigorous, stable, substantial

sour *a.* 1. acid, vinegary, tart, bitter, sharp-tasting, nasty
2. bad-tempered, ill-tempered, surly, sullen

source *n.* origin, beginning

souvenir *n.* memento, keepsake, reminder

space *n.* 1. room, accommodation
2. break, gap
3. infinity, beyond the Earth, the universe
4. period/interval (of time), spell, while

spare *a.* scanty, meager, poor, sparse, lean, thin, insufficient, inadequate
v. 1. do without, use frugally/economically
2. let go, not hurt/harm/kill

sparkle *v.* flash, glitter, glisten, glint, twinkle, gleam, glow, shine, scintillate, shimmer

sparse *a.* scanty, meager, spare, poor, lean, thin, insufficient

speak *v.* talk, say, tell, state, utter, make an address, orate, discourse, express, voice, declare, proclaim

speed *n.* velocity, swiftness, haste, quickness, rapidity, promptness, rate, pace

spell *n.* 1. charm, incantation
2. attraction, fascination
3. period/space (of time), while, interval

spin *v.* revolve, rotate, turn, whirl, twirl, twist

splendid *a.* delightful, superb, fine, grand, magnificent, gorgeous, glorious, excellent, brilliant

spoil *v.* 1. ruin, destroy, damage, harm, hurt, injure, plunder, taint
2. decay, decompose, putrefy, become tainted, rot
n. loot, plunder, booty, prizes

sport *n.* fun, amusement, pastime, game, pursuit, hobby, pleasure, enjoyment, diversion

spread *v.* extend, cover, scatter, distribute, broadcast, transmit, disperse, sow, sprinkle

spring *v.* 1. flow, run, emerge
2. leap, jump, bound
3. recoil, rebound

spy *v.* 1. scout, explore, reconnoiter
2. watch, notice, peer

squabble *v.* quarrel, bicker

squalid *a.* dirty, wretched, miserable, poor, poverty-stricken, disgusting, unpleasant

squeeze *v.* press, crush, grip, clasp, embrace, clutch

squirm *v.* wriggle, writhe, twist

stab *v.* pierce, perforate, puncture, wound

stain *n.* 1. mark, blemish, blot, smear, disfigurement
2. disgrace, dishonor
3. color, dye, paint

stand *v.* 1. be upright/erect
2. maintain, support
3. put up with, endure, abide, suffer
n. 1. stall, booth
2. support, prop, rest
3. firmness, boldness

start *v.* 1. begin, commence, open, initiate
2. go, set/take off, leave, embark

startle *v.* frighten, surprise, shock, alarm, astonish, astound

state *v.* say, relate, describe, tell, voice, express, declare
n. 1. condition, quality
2. country, nation

staunch *a.* steadfast, loyal, trustworthy, faithful, devoted, constant, resolute

stay *v.* remain, rest, abide, linger, loiter, tarry
n. prop, support

steady *a.* 1. regular, continuous, dependable, reliable, constant, steadfast
2. firm, stable, sturdy, still, calm, composed, certain, sure

steal *v.* 1. thieve, burgle, rob, loot, plunder, misappropriate, pilfer, purloin, embezzle
2. lurk, sneak, move/travel silently/unnoticed/slyly/furtively

stern *a.* strict, harsh, severe, unkind, unbending, inflexible

stiff *a.* 1. rigid, firm, solid, unbending, immovable, inflexible
2. not easy, hard, difficult, tough

still *a.* calm, motionless, immobile, steady, tranquil, serene, quiet, peaceful, silent
adv. however, nevertheless, but

stir *v.* move, arouse, rouse, upset, excite, agitate, stimulate

stop *v.* 1. cease, end, quit, finish, terminate
2. arrest, halt, check, block
3. stay, rest, remain, linger, pause
4. wedge, plug, fill

store *n.* 1. supply, accumulation, stock
2. warehouse, shop, magazine, emporium

storm *n.* 1. wind, gale, tempest
2. assault, attack, onslaught
3. bout/fit of anger/fury/rage

story *n.* 1. tale, yarn, account, anecdote, narrative, description
2. lie, falsehood, untruth, fib, exaggeration, fabrication

stout *a.* 1. fat, obese, corpulent, gross, plump
2. firm, strong, sturdy, tough, lasting, durable, well-built
3. resolute, staunch, determined, bold, brave, courageous

straight *a.* 1. level, flat, even, smooth, not bent/curved/crooked
2. tidy, clear, right, correct
3. honest, genuine, upright, candid, open, frank, direct, sincere

strange *a.* unusual, uncommon, queer, odd, peculiar, eccentric, foreign, alien

strict *a.* 1. severe, harsh, stern, unbending, inflexible
2. exact, precise, rigid, accurate

strike *v.* 1. hit, knock, punch, jab, beat, slap, clout
2. refuse to work, withhold labor

strive *v.* struggle, try, attempt, endeavor

strong *a.* 1. powerful, vigorous, robust, sturdy, hardy, virile
2. glaring, brilliant, vivid, dazzling
3. putrid, rotten, decayed

stubborn *a.* obstinate, unbending, unyielding, obdurate, inflexible, headstrong

stumble *v.* stagger, blunder, trip, fall, pitch over

stupid *a.* foolish, silly, absurd, ridiculous, senseless, dull, unintelligent

sturdy *a.* strong, hardy, stalwart, athletic, robust, stout, powerful, vigorous, tough

style *n.* fashion, vogue, mode, manner, way, technique, approach

subdue *v.* overcome, overpower, quell, crush, conquer, suppress, beat, defeat, master, tame, control

subject *n.* 1. citizen, dependent
2. topic, theme

subject *v.* expose, make liable to

succeed *v.* 1. prosper, thrive, flourish
2. follow, inherit

sudden *a.* quick, fast, rapid, swift, speedy, hasty, abrupt, unexpected

suffer *v.* 1. undergo, bear, stand, put up with, endure, abide
2. permit, allow, let, tolerate

sufficient *a.* enough, ample, adequate, plentiful, abundant, copious

suggestion *n.* 1. proposal, plan, scheme, proposition, recommendation
2. hint, inkling, clue

suitable *a.* appropriate, proper, apt, becoming, befitting, fitting, convenient, satisfactory

superb *a.* splendid, marvelous, wonderful, delightful, excellent, magnificent, fine, grand, glorious, gorgeous

supply *v.* provide, equip, furnish, give
n. store, stock

support *v.* 1. aid, assist, help, sustain, provide for, befriend, encourage, defend, follow, cooperate with, back, stand by
2. uphold, hold up, prop

suppose *v.* fancy, imagine, think, believe, guess, assume, presume

sure *a.* 1. certain, convinced, confident, positive
2. safe, reliable, dependable

surly *a.* sullen, sulky, moody

surprise *n.* astonishment, amazement, wonder, shock, bewilderment

surprised *a.* startled, shocked, astonished, amazed, astounded, stunned, alarmed, bewildered, flabbergasted, taken aback

surrender *v.* give in/up, yield, submit, hand over, capitulate, succumb

surround *v.* hem in, encircle, enclose

surroundings *n.* environment, locale, neighborhood

suspicious *a.* doubtful, dubious, questionable, distrustful, mistrustful

sweet *a.* sugary, pleasant, luscious, fragrant, melodious, pleasing, agreeable, fresh, wholesome
n. candy, confection, sweetmeat

swell *v.* grow bigger/bolder/larger, increase, enlarge, inflate, expand, bulge, bloat

swift *a.* quick, fast, rapid, speedy, hasty, hurried, fleet

sympathy *n.* understanding, fellow-feeling, compassion

system *n.* 1. regular method/way, structure, organization, order, plan, scheme, arrangement
2. human body/frame

T t

tab *n.* flap, tongue, tag, label, tally

table *n.* 1. list/summary (of facts/figures), chart
2. flat top, board, slab
3. level area, plain, plateau

tactful *a.* prudent, discreet, diplomatic, cautious, careful

taint *v.* spoil, blemish, soil, sully, stain, infect, decay, decompose, putrefy, corrupt

take *v.* 1. remove, abstract, subtract, receive, grasp, seize, arrest, capture
2. lead, conduct, escort

tale *n.* story, yarn, account, anecdote, narrative

talent *n.* skill, ability, aptitude, gift

talk *v.* speak, say, tell, chatter, gossip, discourse, converse, discuss, address, expound, orate

talkative *a.* chatty, voluble, garrulous, loquacious

tall *a.* high, lofty, elevated, steep, towering

tame *a.* timid, docile, subdued, gentle, obedient, not wild, domesticated

tasteful *a.* good, pleasing, artistic, stylish, elegant

tasty *a.* delicious, savory, piquant, appetizing, sweet, luscious

teach *v.* instruct, train, discipline, tutor, coach, educate, inform

tease *v.* annoy, irritate, disturb, torment, plague, tantalize, taunt, aggravate

tedious *a.* tiresome, wearisome, fatiguing, monotonous, boring, dull

tell *v.* say, relate, speak, state, inform, express, voice, disclose, announce, reveal, mention

tempt *v.* entice, lure, invite, attract, charm, enchant, captivate, beguile

tender *a.* 1. soft, gentle, mild, delicate, fragile
2. kind, loving, sympathetic, compassionate
3. sore, painful, aching

v. offer, volunteer

terminate *v.* end, finish, close, complete, conclude

terrible *a.* dreadful, frightful, horrid, frightening, horrible, shocking, awful, terrifying

terrific *a.* terrible, awful, frightening, terrifying, huge, immense, enormous, gigantic, tremendous

terrified *a.* in terror, very afraid/frightened/scared/alarmed

terror *n.* great fear/fright/alarm, dread, horror

test *v.* try, examine, check, inspect, investigate

thankful *a.* grateful, obliged, indebted

theft *n.* robbery, stealing, pilfering, burglary, larceny, piracy

thick *a.* 1. crowded, swarming, packed, close rank, dense, plentiful, numerous
2. deep, not thin, broad

thin *a.* 1. not fat, lean, slender, slight, slim, narrow, lanky, gaunt, scrawny, skinny
2. meager, scanty, skimpy, insufficient, inadequate

think *v.* 1. reason, ponder, consider, meditate, reflect
2. imagine, fancy, believe

thorough *a.* complete, entire, full, perfect, exact, accurate

thought *n.* belief, idea, notion, view, opinion

thrash *v.* beat, belabor, chastise

threaten *v.* warn, menace, intimidate, imperil

throw *v.* hurl, fling, heave, cast, sling, toss, pitch

tidy *a.* neat, clean, orderly, trim

tight *a.* stretched, taut, not elastic, secure, firm, steady

tilt *v.* slope, slant, incline, lean over

timid *a.* tame, shy, reticent, retiring, afraid, apprehensive

tiny *a.* very small/little, minute, wee, trifling, trivial, insignificant

tip *v.* 1. tilt, turn over, upset
2. reward, recompense

tire *v.* weary, fatigue, exhaust, bore

tiresome *a.* wearisome, boring, tedious, irritating, annoying

toil *v.* work, labor, strive, slave

tolerate *v.* put up with, allow, let, permit, bear, suffer, abide, overlook, stand for

top *n.* highest point/part, summit, head, crown, crest, zenith

torment *v.* torture, persecute, tease, badger, plague, distress, annoy, irritate

tough *a.* hard, durable, strong, powerful, sturdy, robust, firm,. stubborn

tow *v.* tug, pull, haul

trace *v.* 1. seek and find, trail, track, discover
2. mark, copy, reproduce

tradition *n.* custom, belief

tragic *a.* disastrous, calamitous, sad, sorrowful, unfortunate

train *v.* teach, instruct, rear, educate, exercise, bring up, discipline, prepare

tranquil *a.* peaceful, calm, composed, untroubled, undisturbed, serene, restful, quiet, still

transform *v.* change, alter, convert, turn

transport *v.* 1. carry, convey, bring
2. delight, enrapture

trap *n.* 1. snare, ambush, pitfall
2. plot, trick, deception
v. catch, capture, snare

travel *v.* journey, voyage, move, proceed, progress

treachery *n.* disloyalty, betrayal, deceit, trickery

treat *v.* 1. handle, manage, deal with
2. please, favor, delight

treaty *n.* agreement, compact, truce, contract

tremble *v.* shake, shiver, shudder, quake, quiver, quaver

tremendous *a.* immense, huge, gigantic, enormous, vast, colossal, awe-inspiring

trick *v.* 1. puzzle, deceive, baffle, mystify, hoax
2. swindle, cheat, defraud

tricky *a.* 1. artful, crafty, cunning, deceitful, deceptive
2. difficult, risky, dangerous

trip *n.* journey, voyage, tour, expedition, outing

triumph *n.* success, achievement, victory, win, conquest

trivial *a.* trifling, small, little, paltry, petty, slight, insignificant, unimportant

trouble *n.* 1. bother, worry, vexation, predicament, plight, disaster, distress, calamity
2. care, effort, pains
v. disturb, pester, irritate, molest, distress, upset, annoy, perturb

true *a.* 1. real, genuine, actual, authentic
2. faithful, loyal, reliable, devoted, trustworthy, constant, sincere

trust *n.* belief, faith, fidelity, hope, confidence, reliance

trustworthy *a.* upright, reliable, faithful, loyal, dependable, honest, truthful

truth *n.* honesty, candor, frankness, accuracy

try *v.* 1. test, check, examine
2. attempt, endeavor, tackle

tune *n.* melody, harmony, song, air

turn *v.* 1. change, alter, convert
2. revolve, rotate, roll, spin, whirl, twirl, twist

twist *v.* 1. wind, turn, rotate, twirl, whirl
2. curve, bend, change the shape of, contort, distort

tyrant *n.* overbearing/cruel master/ overseer/overlord, oppressor, despot, dictator

U u

ugly *a.* 1. not beautiful/handsome/pretty/lovely, unattractive, unpleasing, repulsive, unsightly, hideous
2. unpleasant, threatening, ill-natured, sinister, dangerous, vile

unable *a.* not able, not capable, incapable, powerless

unaware *a.* unconscious, without knowledge, unknowing, ignorant, uninformed

uncertain *a.* doubtful, dubious, insecure, unsure, undecided, indefinite, unsettled

uncivil *a.* impolite, discourteous, rude, bad-mannered, unmannerly

unclean *a.* dirty, grimy, tainted, blemished, sullied, soiled, polluted, filthy, foul

uncomfortable *a.* disagreeable, uneasy, displeasing, unsure, uneasy

uncommon *a.* rare, unusual, remarkable, extraordinary

unconcerned *a.* not bothered, unmoved, indifferent, nonchalant

uncouth *a.* vulgar, common, rude. boorish, loutish, coarse, ill-mannered, bad-mannered, without courtesy/breeding/quality/dignity, clumsy, awkward

uncover *v.* reveal, disclose, unclothe, disrobe, make bare/naked/nude

undecided *a.* doubtful, dubious, hesitating, hesitant, irresolute, wavering, unsure, uncertain, unsettled

under *prep.* beneath, below, inferior to, lower than

undergo *v.* experience, put up with, bear, suffer, endure, be subjected to

underhand *a.* deceitful, treacherous, sly, crafty, cunning, secret, fraudulent, not straight/straightforward/aboveboard

understand *v.* comprehend, know, grasp, appreciate, perceive, infer

undeserved *a.* unmerited, unearned, not deserved

undiscovered *a.* hidden, not found, unfound, undisclosed, unrevealed

undisturbed *a.* untroubled, cool, calm, confident, sanguine

undoubted *a.* not doubtful, certain, sure, undeniable, concrete, absolute

unearth *v.* discover, find, uncover, disclose, reveal, recover

uneasy *a.* not confident, unsettled, restless, agitated, fidgety, worried, bothered, troubled, concerned, anxious, disturbed, uncomfortable

unequal *a.* uneven, unmatched, irregular, unbalanced, different, not alike/the same

unequaled *a.* matchless, without peer

uneven *a.* rough, coarse, matte, irregular, lopsided, bumpy, undulating

unexpected *a.* unforeseen, surprising, unusual

unfair *a.* partial, unjust, wrong, wrongful, incorrect, improper, biased

unfaithful *a.* disloyal, untrue, deceitful, treacherous, unreliable, untrustworthy

unfasten *v.* undo, untie, unbind, unfetter, disconnect, set loose, free, release

unfit *a.* 1. unsuitable, inappropriate, improper, unqualified, untrained
2. unwell, ill, ailing, sick, bad, unhealthy

unfortunate *a.* unlucky, ill-fated, ill-starred, unsuccessful

unfriendly *a.* hostile, antagonistic, cold, unreceptive

ungrateful *a.* thankless, unthankful, without gratitude

unhappy *a.* sad, miserable, sorrowful, gloomy, discontented, dejected, doleful, dismal, distressed, depressed, downcast, despondent

uniform *a.* equal, even, the same, similar, alike, constant, regular, consistent, unchanging, fixed, steady, not varied
n. dress, costume (of soldier, sailor, policeman, etc.)

unimportant *a.* small, slight, trivial, commonplace, mediocre, average, humble, nondescript, insignificant

unit *n.* 1. one, thing, item, object, article, part, piece, section, group
2. measure

unite *v.* join together, combine, amalgamate, bind, marry, fasten/tie together, become one

universal *a.* general, widespread, known everywhere, worldwide, international

unjust *a.* unfair, incorrect, wrong, wrongful, improper, biased

unkind *a.* uncharitable, ungenerous, intolerant, spiteful, vindictive, harsh, cruel

unknown *a.* undiscovered, unfound, unexplored, anonymous

unlikely *a.* improbable, unsuitable

unlucky *a.* unfortunate, ill-fated, unsuccessful

unnecessary *a.* unneeded, needless, unwanted, unrequired

unreasonable *a.* irrational, illogical, absurd, not sensible

unreliable *a.* not dependable, disloyal, unfaithful, untrustworthy

unruly *a.* disorderly, undisciplined, disobedient, rowdy, unmanageable

unsatisfactory *a.* unsuitable, inappropriate, displeasing, substandard, scratch

unskilled *a.* unskillful, inexpert, untalented, untrained, incompetent

untidy *a.* disordered, slovenly, scruffy, unkempt, disheveled

until *prep.* till, up to, to the time of

untrue *a.* 1. inaccurate, incorrect, false, counterfeit, erroneous, dishonest
2. unfaithful, disloyal, faithless

unusual *a.* not commonplace/ordinary, uncommon, strange, odd, peculiar, eccentric

unwise *a.* without wisdom/sagacity/foresight, foolish, rash, reckless, unthinking

unworthy *a.* undeserving, dishonorable

upright *a.* 1. vertical, perpendicular, erect, straight up
2. honest, true, trustworthy, straight

uproar *n.* row, commotion, disturbance, chaos

upset *v.* 1. overturn, topple, knock over, disturb
2. agitate, bother, worry, trouble, be concerned

urge *v.* push, press, drive, impel, prod, hasten, beg, beseech, entreat, exhort, pray, implore

urgent *a.* pressing, in need of immediate attention, important, serious, grave

use *v.*
1. employ, utilize, apply, treat
2. consume, exhaust, wear out

useful *a.* helpful, advantageous, profitable, gainful, valuable, serviceable

useless *a.* ineffectual, unprofitable, ineffective, futile

usual *a.* common, ordinary, normal, general, regular, customary

utmost *a.* farthest, most distant, greatest, strongest, extreme, uttermost

utter *v.* speak, say, voice, declare, assert, blurt, articulate, pronounce, murmur

a. complete, total, absolute, sheer, pure, unadulterated, extreme, entire

uttermost *a.* farthest, most distant, greatest, strongest, utmost

V v

vacant *a.* 1. empty, unfilled, deserted, unoccupied, vacated, given up, left open, free
2. dreamy, stupid, foolish, empty-headed, thoughtless, not mentally occupied, not alert/wide-awake

vacate *v.* leave, quit, depart from, give up, abandon, forsake, cease to occupy, go out of, desert

vacation *n.* holiday, holiday-time, absence (from work), leave, furlough (soldiers)

vagabond *n.* idle wanderer, tramp, rogue, rascal, scoundrel, scamp, harum-scarum, scapegrace, scallywag

vague *a.* not clear, indistinct, obscure, ambiguous, uncertain, unsure, indefinite, indeterminate, unsettled, confusing, confused, doubtful, dubious, nebulous, hazy, misty, formless, shapeless, dim

vain *a.* 1. proud, conceited, bumptious, pompous, egotistical, self-centered, self-satisfied, boastful, self-opinionated, bombastic, vainglorious
2. useless, pointless, futile, purposeless, needless, unnecessary, trivial, insubstantial, empty
in vain: *without value/result/reason/purpose*

valiant *a.* brave, courageous, fearless, valorous, dauntless, heroic, undaunted, dashing, daring, gallant, bold, unafraid

valley *n.* vale, dale, depression, hollow

value *n.* 1. importance, usefulness, utility, worth, merit, quality, esteem, appreciation, estimation, assessment, appraisal, desirability
2. cost, price, charge, estimate, computation

van *n.* 1. cart, truck, wagon, coach, carriage
2. advance part, front (of an army or fleet), vanguard

vanish *v.* disappear, go/pass out of sight, become invisible, fade away, dissolve, evaporate

vanquish *v.* conquer, defeat, beat, be victorious, triumph over, subdue, quell, overcome, overpower, master, quell

variety *n.* type, sort, kind, form, class, character, assortment, selection, variation, difference, diversity

various *a.* several, a number of, more than one, sundry, miscellaneous, diverse, different, varied, separate

vast *a.* very large, great, huge, enormous, gigantic, boundless

vehicle *n.* carriage, conveyance/medium/means for land transport

velocity *n.* speed, swiftness, rate, quickness, rapidity, haste, fleetness, pace

vend *v.* sell, offer for sale, trade/deal in, retail, peddle

vengeance *n.* revenge, retribution, vindictiveness

venture *n.* dangerous undertaking, daring/risky exploit/enterprise/project, adventure

verbal *a.* oral, vocal, spoken, said, voiced, unwritten

verdict *n.* decision, judgement, finding, conclusion, opinion, jury's finding/conclusion/judgement/answer

verify *v.* check, examine, test, prove truth/honesty/accuracy/soundness/value/facts of, confirm, bear out

versatile *a.* adaptable, adjustable, changeable, moving freely, capable of/competent in doing many things

vertical *a.* perpendicular, upright, straight up, erect

vessel *n.* 1. container, receptacle, jar, pot, urn, pitcher, beaker, jug, bottle, flask, flagon, phial, vial, pan, can, bin, cask
2. ship, boat

vex *v.* anger, annoy, make irate, provoke, irritate, trouble, afflict, grieve

vibrate *v.* tremble, twitch, shudder, shake, quake, quiver, quaver, rock, agitate, throb, buzz, resound, resonate

vice *n.* wickedness, immorality, wrongdoing, evil, vileness, malignity, malpractice, bad habit, sin, sinfulness, depravity, debauchery, profligacy, license, corruption, fault, defect, blemish

vicious *a.* wicked, immoral, wrongful, evil, vile, malignant, sinful, depraved, distasteful, odious, noxious, corrupt, injurious, spiteful, very unkind, ill-tempered, aggressive, violent, savage, defective, blemished

victim *n.* wrongfully-used person/animal, sufferer, quarry, prey, dupe, gull

victory *n.* conquest, triumph, success, mastery, win, gain, achievement, attainment

view *n.* 1. scene, sight, observation, outlook, setting, vista, panorama
2. opinion, attitude, aim, purpose, intention

v. see, observe, watch, look at/on, regard, survey, scan, inspect, examine

birds-eye view: *overhead view, plan*

viewpoint *n.* standpoint, point of view, opinion, attitude

vigilant *a.* watchful, attentive, wide-awake, alert, aware, cautious, careful, wary, circumspect

vigorous *a.* lively, alive, quick-moving, spry, nimble, energetic, lusty, strenuous, active, animated, brisk, effective, strong, forceful, hard, sharp, powerful, strong, robust, healthy, flourishing, spirited

vile *a.* evil, guilty, wicked, immoral, malignant, sinful, very bad, odious, depraved, corrupt, unpleasant, loathsome, repulsive, distasteful, worthless, base, abject

villain *n.* guilty person, scoundrel, criminal, rogue, rascal, vagabond, wrongdoer, scallywag

violate *v.* 1. attack, despoil, injure, disturb, profane, desecrate, act against, break, treat roughly/badly/unkindly/wrongly/rudely, damage, pollute
2. transgress, infringe

violent *a.* forceful, powerful, strong, intense, passionate, vehement, turbulent, raging, angry, furious, fierce, unruly, vindictive, savage, brutal, cruel, aggressive, barbarous, barbaric

virile *a.* strong, active, energetic, vigorous, powerful, healthy, full of life, manly, procreative

virtue *n.* goodness, excellence, rectitude, righteousness, straightness, purity, morality, good quality, inherent quality/power

visible *a.* can be seen/observed/distinguished/identified, plain, clear, discernible, detectable

vision *n.* 1. eyesight, perception, discernment
2. imagined sight, image, dream, fantasy, phantom, spirit, ghost, apparition, wraith, specter
3. foresight, insight, ideal, wisdom, sagacity

visit *v.* go/come to see, call upon, stay with, frequent

visitation *n.* official visit, inspection, long visit, social call, dispensation

vital *a.* necessary to/needed for life/existence, very important, essential, much needed

vivacious *a.* lively, alive, spirited, sprightly, animated, gay, bright

vivid *a.* very clear, glaring, bright, brilliant, intense, strong, forceful, powerful, striking, vigorous, vibrant, unforgettable, true to life

vocal *a.* voiced, spoken, said, sung, oral, verbal, vociferous

vogue *n.* fashion, mode, popular use/reception/acceptance, present/prevailing/current custom/practice

voice *v.* litter, speak, say, express, declare
n. say, wish, viewpoint, point of view, opinion

void *a.* empty, vacant, useless, ineffectual, lacking, cancelled, null, invalid, not binding
v. quit, emit, discharge, evacuate

volume *n.* 1. capacity, content, size, bulk, mass
2. a roll of parchment, a scroll
3. book, tome

volunteer *v.* offer, make a voluntary offer, put forward, undertake, elect, choose

vote *n.* ballot, show of hands, election

vouch *v.* confirm, bear witness, uphold, guarantee, certify, be surety, underwrite,

vow *n.* promise, oath, engagement, undertaking, pledge

voyage *n.* sea journey, cruise

vulgar *a.* common, prevalent, ill-mannered, bad-mannered, without taste/quality/manners/breeding, undignified, discourteous, coarse, uncouth, rude, loutish, boorish, plebeian

vulnerable *a.* easily wounded/assaulted/attacked/hurt/assailed, assailable, susceptible to injury, liable to danger, unsafe, unprotected, undefended

Ww

wage *v.* carry on, conduct (a war)

wager *v.* bet, gamble, back, pledge, promise

wages *n.* wage, pay, payment, salary, earnings, income, stipend

wait *v.* 1. stay, stop, rest, remain, tarry, linger, loiter
2. await, wait/look/watch for, expect, anticipate

waken *v.* awaken, awake, wake up, rouse, arouse, stir, bestir

wander *v.* stray, roam, ramble, meander, stroll, saunter, amble, digress

wane *v.* weaken, diminish, lessen, fail, sink, ebb

want *v.* 1. desire, wish/crave/long/yearn for
2. lack, need, require
n. 1. desire, wish, craving, longing, yearning
2. shortage, omission, scarcity, need, poverty, deficiency
in want: *in need, destitute*

warn *v.* give notice, caution, inform/advise/notify of danger, alarm, admonish, threaten

warp *v.* 1. twist, distort, spoil, disfigure
2. haul, tow (a ship)

wary *a.* careful, cautious, wise, prudent, alert, vigilant, watchful

waste *v.* 1. use/spend unnecessarily/unprofitably/extravagantly, squander, spoil
2. wither, decay, fade
n. 1. rubbish, refuse, junk, trumpery
2. extravagance, improvidence
3. desert, wilderness

wasteful *a.* extravagant, improvident, lavish, thriftless, unthrifty, destructive

watch *v.* 1. observe, look at, notice, be alert/vigilant/attentive
2. guard, take care of, protect

waver *v.* hesitate, be uncertain, demur, vacillate, prevaricate, falter, pause

wax *v.* strengthen, increase, expand, enlarge

way *n.* 1. path, road, route, track, direction
2. method, technique, plan, style, fashion, mode, vogue
by the way: *by the by, incidentally*

wayward *a.* perverse, contrary, awkward, difficult, precocious

weak *a.* 1. not strong/robust/powerful, feeble, frail, delicate, fragile, sickly, infirm
2. easily influenced, irresolute, shallow

wealth *n.* riches, money, fortune, abundance, prosperity, affluence, resources, capital, assets

weary *a.* tired, fatigued, exhausted, worn, jaded
v. tire, fatigue, exhaust, wear

weep *v.* cry, shed tears, sob

weird *a.* strange, odd, peculiar, mysterious, uncanny, eerie, unearthly

wet *a.* sloppy, sodden, soaked, drenched, moist, damp, humid

whim *n.* fancy, idea, notion, craze, caprice

whirl *v.* spin, rotate, revolve, turn

white *a.* 1. pale, pallid, ashen, snowy
2. spotless, clean

whole *a.* 1. complete, total, full, entire, undivided
2. sound, perfect, healthy

wicked *a.* 1. evil, sinful, malevolent, malignant, vile, corrupt
2. naughty, mischievous, roguish, bad

wide *a.* broad, extensive, vast, spacious

wild *a.* 1. not tame/domesticated/timid/orderly, untamed, undomesticated, disorderly, savage barbaric, uncivilized
2. waste, uncultivated, uninhabited

wilderness *n.* desert, waste, barren/infertile/uncultivated/uninhabited land

willful *a.* 1. deliberate, intentional
2. obstinate, self-willed, perverse, awkward, stubborn, determined

win *v.* get, obtain, gain, earn, acquire, come to possess/own, capture, secure, achieve, procure

wind *n.* breeze, gust, blow, gale, air current, draught, breath

wīnd *v.* turn, twist, curve, bend, meander, coil, reel

wise *a.* sagacious, sensible, clever, intelligent, profound, well-informed, prudent
n. way, manner, method, approach

wish *v.* want, desire, crave, long, hope, yearn
n. desire, craving, longing, yearning, hope

wit *n.* 1. intelligence, sense, wisdom, understanding, shrewdness, intellect
2. wittiness, humor

withdraw *v.* 1. go/come away from, retire, retreat, leave, pull/draw out/back, remove
2. recall, take back words/accusation/opinion

withstand *v.* resist, oppose

wonder *v.* 1. marvel, be amazed/surprised/astonished/bewildered
2. doubt, consider, speculate

wonderful *a.* marvellous, amazing, astounding, surprising, inspiring, fine, grand, splendid, superb, spectacular, striking, magnificent, awesome

woo *v.* court, ask in marriage

work *n.* 1. labor, effort, toil, task, production
2. job, employment, trade, business, occupation, profession, vocation, calling
3. achievement, feat, deed, product

worn *a.* 1. used, threadbare, ragged, shabby
2. tired, fatigued, weary, exhausted, jaded

worry *v.* bother, trouble, disturb, irritate, tease, tantalize, torment, annoy, sadden
n. problem, care, anxiety, burden

worship *v.* revere, respect, idolize, venerate, praise, laud, glorify, adore, deify

worth *n.* value, cost, price, merit, excellence, importance, benefit

worthless *a.* of no worth/value/merit, without worth/value/merit/excellence, valueless, useless, pointless

worthy *a.* honest, true, upright, decent, righteous, good, worthwhile, admirable, excellent

wound *v.* hurt, injure, maim, upset, grieve

wrath *n.* anger, rage, fury, ire, vexation, annoyance, indignation

wreck *v.* 1. ruin, destroy, disable, blight, spoil
2. be shipwrecked
n. 1. ruined/emaciated/dissipated/unhealthy person
2. shipwreck, wrecked ship

wreckage *n.* remains, debris, remnants, fragments, flotsam

wretched *a.* 1. sad, dejected, miserable, unhappy, afflicted, woeful, discontented, pathetic, pitiful, pitiable
2. mean, contemptible, unworthy, despised, shabby, poor, impoverished

writhe *v.* 1. twist, wriggle, squirm, reel, roll
2. be stung/annoyed

wrong *a.* 1. wrongful, not right, incorrect, inaccurate, improper, unsuitable
2. bad, wicked, immoral, evil, vicious, sinful, unjust, unfair, illegal, unlawful
n. injury, misdeed, sin, evil, vice, wickedness, injustice
v. injure, damage, hurt, harm, abuse, treat unfairly/unjustly

wry *a.* twisted, crooked, distorted, askew
awry: *crookedly, distortedly*

X x

Xmas *n.* (abbreviation for) Christmas, the Christmas season, Christmas-tide, Christmas-time, the Christmas feast/festival, yule, yule-tide

X-rays *n.* penetrating rays, Roentgen rays
X-ray: *X-ray examination/photograph*

Y y

yank *v.* jerk, pull sharply/quickly/suddenly/forcibly/forcefully, snatch

yarn *n.* story, tale, anecdote, account, narrative

yearn *v.* long, crave, desire greatly/strongly, want very much, wish, hanker, pine

yell *v.* bawl, cry out/loudly/shrilly, shout loudly/suddenly, scream, blare, blast

yelp *n.* loud yap, shrill bark, sharp/loud cry

yet *adv.*
1. still, until/up to then/now, this/the present time, at present, at that/this time, so far, in the near future
2. also, in addition, again, further
3. however, nevertheless, despite that/this, in spite of that/this, but for all that, but at the same time

yield *v.*
1. give up/in, surrender, submit, relinquish, resign, hand/deliver over
2. give, produce, supply, provide, deliver

n. product, supply, output, amount/quantity produced, crop, harvest

young *a.* youthful, juvenile, not adult/grown-up, immature

youngster *n.* child, juvenile, young person, minor

youth *n.* young man, teenage boy/lad, male adolescent

yule *n.* yuletide, Christmas (Xmas), Christmas-tide, Christmas-time, the Christmas feast/festival/season

Z z

zeal *n.* enthusiasm, eagerness, ardor, passion, devotion, determination, keenness, fervor, fanaticism, earnestness, zest, verve, vigor, intensity

zealot *n.* zealous person, fanatic, extremist

zero *n.* 1. nothing, nought, nil
2. startingpoint (on a scale)
3. figure *0*, cipher
zero-hour: *1. twelve o'clock (midnight)*
2. fixed/pre-arranged starting-time

zest *n.* great enjoyment, keen interest, relish, gusto, enthusiasm, eagerness, passion, keenness, fervor, zeal, vigor, vim, verve, vivacity

zigzag *a.* with alternate right and left turns/angles, with a series of sharp bends, jagged, barbed, twisted, crooked, winding

zip *n.* 1. energy, vigor, verve, rapid action, fast movement, great motion, high speed, zest, vim, vivacity
2. light/sharp/bullet-like/tearing sound
3. zip-fastener

zone *n.* belt, girdle, space, region
It is extremely cold in Earth's frigid **zones**.

zoom *v.* move/climb noisily and speedily
The airplane **zoomed** into the clouds.

Supplement
Opposites

abandon 1. keep, retain, hold, remain in, occupy, take over 2. restraint, caution, care
abandoned 1. kept, retained, occupied, owned 2. restrained, restricted, cautious
abate increase, strengthen, begin, start
abduct 1. return 2. care for, protect, guard
abhor like, love, admire, cherish
abide 1. go/depart from 2. reject, dismiss
ability inability, incompetence, inefficiency
able unable, incompetent, ineffective, weak
abnormal normal, usual, regular, ordinary
abolish establish, validate, allow, permit
above below, beneath, lower than, under
aboveboard dishonest, deceitful, suspicious
abroad near, here, not distant, at home
abrupt gradual, slow, gentle, courteous
absent present, here, in existence
absolute imperfect, incomplete, restricted
absorb exude, emit, give off/out
abstain participate, indulge/join in
abstract real, concrete, feasible, practical
absurd sound, sensible, logical, reasonable
abundance scarcity, shortage, paucity
abuse care for, treat properly, respect
accelerate decelerate, slow down, retard, impede
accept reject, refuse, decline, dismiss
access way out, exit, outlet
accommodate not help/serve, hinder, withhold
accompany disregard, ignore, avoid
accomplice enemy, opponent, adversary
accomplish fail, give up/in, relinquish
accumulate disperse, scatter, lose, spend
accurate inaccurate, inexact, doubtful
achieve fail, lose, give up, forsake
acknowledge 1. ignore 2. deny, refuse, reject
acquaint conceal, keep confidential
acquire lose, give away, reject, refuse
action inactivity, inaction, laziness
active inactive, slow, idle, slothful
actual unreal, abstract, false, fictitious
acute obtuse, low, soft, mild, dull
adamant yielding, resilient, flexible
add subtract, deduct, decrease, remove
adequate inadequate, insufficient, not enough
adhere be separated/loosened/detached
adjacent far, distant, detached, apart, separate
adjust disarrange, disorder
admire disapprove, dislike, condemn
admit deny, disallow, repudiate
adopt disown, forsake, abandon, desert
adore dislike, detest, hate, abhor, loathe
adrift fixed, moored, tied-up, fastened
adult 1. child, youngster 2. immature, childish
advance 1. withdraw, retreat 2. decline, worsen
advantage disadvantage, hindrance, handicap
adversary friend, ally, accomplice, assistant
advertise conceal, hide, camouflage, cover up, disguise
affection dislike, hatred, aversion, abhorrence
afford 1. unable to buy 2. withhold
afloat sunk, on shore, not at sea
afraid brave, courageous, bold, fearless
age 1. youth 2. rejuvenate
agile awkward, slow, sluggish, clumsy
agitate calm, quiet, soothe, relieve
agony joy, gladness, pleasure, delight
agree disagree, refuse, oppose, disapprove
agreeable disagreeable, unpleasant, nasty
agreement disagreement, opposition
ahead behind, retarded, late, tardy
aid 1. hindrance, opposition 2. hinder, impede
alarm 1. calm, peace 2. soothe, quiet, pacify, console
alert 1. inattentive, dreamy, absentminded 2. sluggish, slow, inactive, lethargic
alight fly off, ascend, mount, get on
alike not alike/the same, dissimilar, different
allow disallow, forbid, ban, refuse, deny
alone accompanied/in company
alter preserve, keep, maintain, retain
amateur expert, master, specialist, professional
ambition aimlessness, indifference, disinterest
amend spoil, destroy, injure, impair
amiable unfriendly, ill-tempered, moody
ample inadequate, insufficient, short, deficient
amuse displease, bore, weary

anger please, delight, charm, amuse
announce conceal, hide, withhold, cover up
annoy please, amuse, charm, soothe
answer 1. question, query 2. ask, request
anticipate neglect, forget, disregard
anxiety peace, calm, contentment
apart together, adjacent, close, near
apparent 1. real, actual 2. doubtful, unlikely
appeal deny, refuse, repudiate
appear disappear, vanish
applaud condemn, disapprove, decry
appreciation 1. disapproval, misunderstanding 2. depreciation, fall in value
approach departure, way out, exit
appropriate inappropriate, unsuitable
approve disapprove, condemn, decry
apt 1. inappropriate, unsuitable 2. badly put/chosen, unimpressive
argue agree, concur, consent
arouse calm, quiet, soothe, mollify
arrange disarrange, disorder, scatter
arrest release, let go, free
ascend descend, fall, come/go down
ashamed unashamed, unabashed
ask reply, retort, answer, tell
assault retreat, withdrawal
assemble dismiss, disperse, scatter
assist hinder, impede, delay
associate 1. disassociate, compete 2. competitor, rival
assume relinquish, give up, avoid
astray 1. on course, direct 2. found
attach detach, unfasten, sever, disconnect
attachment dislike, aversion, animosity
attack retreat, withdraw, fall back
attain fail, lose, fall short of
attempt avoid, evade, shirk, disregard
attend ignore, disregard, be absent from
attire disrobe, undress, unclothe
attract repel, repulse, displease
audacity timidity, shyness, reticence
authentic unreliable, sham, false
avail hinder, impede, delay
available out of reach, distant, inconvenient
avarice generosity, unselfishness, benevolence
average unusual, exceptional, out of the ordinary, uncommon, extraordinary
aversion love, fondness, affection
avert accept, receive, tolerate
avoid accept, receive, meet, confront, frequent
awake 1. fall asleep 2. asleep, sleeping
aware unconscious, unaware, unknowing
away near, close, here, present, at home
awe irreverence, disrespect, indifference
awkward 1. graceful, elegant 2. easy, simple
babyish adult, mature, grown-up
back 1. front, fore part, front side 2. advance, progress 3. hinder, impede
backward 1. beforehand, forward, in advance 2. bright, smart, intelligent
bad 1. good, obedient, moral, virtuous 2. rich, superior, pleasing, pure 3. well, healthy
baffle enlighten, instruct, inform
balance 1. imbalance 2. make unequal
ban allow, permit, tolerate, institute
band single, lone, individual
banish call/bring back, recall
bar allow, permit, tolerate, accept
bare covered, clothed, adorned, ample
barely amply, sufficiently, quite
barren fruitful, fertile, full, profitable
base 1. top, summit 2. admirable, noble
bashful forward, bold, brazen
battle peace, agreement, truce
bear 1. collapse under 2. disallow
beautiful ugly, unattractive, repulsive
become 1. remain, cease to be 2. ill adorn
becoming unsuitable, inappropriate, unbecoming
before after, behind, late
befriend alienate, be hostile to, hinder
beg give, allow, grant, consider
beggarly 1. abundant, adequate 2. rich, wealthy
begin cease, finish, end, terminate
behind before, beforehand, in advance, ahead, in good time
belief disbelief, doubt, uncertainty
belong not belong, be separate/apart, inapplicable
below above, on top, superior to, higher than
bend straighten, level, unbend
beneath above, higher than, superior to

benefit disadvantage, burden, loss
benevolent unhelpful, miserly, ill-disposed
beside distant/far/apart from, detached, separate
best worst, most unsuitable/debased
better worse, less preferable/desirable
bewilder enlighten, instruct, inform
beyond near, close, here, inside
bicker agree, concur, consent
big small, little, trivial, unimportant
bind unbind, unfasten, untie, set free
bitter sweet, luscious, pleasing, pleasant
blame praise, commend, applaud
blank full, occupied, written/printed on
blatant quiet, peaceful, disguised, concealed
bleak bright, brilliant, interesting, attractive
blend disunite, separate, disharmonize
blessed cursed, defiled, unfortunate, ill-favored
blind 1. seeing 2. knowing, aware, appreciative
block open, empty, support, help
bloodthirsty peaceful, tame, civilized
blunder diplomatic/sensible/correct/wise act/action
blurred distinct, clear, unstained
boast humility, reticence
bogus genuine, real, true, authentic
bold timid, shy, nervous, afraid
bondage freedom, liberty
bore interest, amuse, entertain, beguile
borrow lend, provide a loan, give, impart
boundless bounded, limited, restricted, finite
bravado timidity, humility, modesty
brave afraid, frightened, cowardly
brawny skinny, weak, frail
break 1. join, unite 2. mend, repair
brief long, lengthy, comprehensive
bright 1. dull, dim, faded 2. backward, slow
brilliant 1. dull, drab 2. retarded, stupid
bring leave, take, remove, return
brisk slow, lazy, idle, retarded
brittle strong, secure, tough, durable
broad narrow, slender, slim, closed
broadcast gather, collect, assemble
brutal kind, considerate, merciful
build dismantle, demolish, destroy
bully encourage, soothe, protect
bumptious humble, meek, modest, unpretentious
burn extinguish, put out
busy inactive, unoccupied, unemployed, dilatory, idle
buy sell, vend, peddle
call listen, hear, attend
calm disturbed, agitated, upset, uneasy
camouflage reveal, expose, uncover, display
cancel allow, keep, approve, support
capable incapable, incompetent, inefficient
capture free, release, liberate, rescue
care 1. neglect, carelessness, unconcern 2. unwariness, imprudence
careless careful, cautious, thoughtful, mindful
carry release, put down, drop
cast 1. catch, grab, pick up 2. deform, misshape
casual careful, cautious, formal, orderly
catch 1. cast, throw 2. miss 3. release, rescue
cause 1. effect, result 2. prevent
cautious incautious, careless, unwary, imprudent
cease begin, commence, start, initiate
ceaseless ceasing, ending, interrupted
celebrate disregard, ignore, overlook, forget
center outside, exterior, external part
certain uncertain, unsure, indefinite
challenge agreement, acceptance, compliance
champion 1. loser 2. rival 3. poorest, worst
chance certainty, design
change remain, keep, maintain
chaos order, system, method
charge 1. withdrawal, retreat 2. praise, commend, excuse, pardon charm repel, displease, disenchant
cheap costly, dear, high-priced, valuable
cheat protect, cover, be honest with
check 1. speed up, accelerate 2. ignore, disregard
cheek respect, regard, consideration
cheer 1. displease, dishearten, discourage 2. jeer, decry, condemn
chief 1. unimportant, insignificant 2. follower, subordinate
child adult, grown-up, mature person
chill 1. hot, warm 2. friendly, emotional
choose ignore, disregard, disown

claim reject, disregard, disown
clamp unclasp, release, free
clean dirty, soiled, impure, untidy
clear indistinct, dull, dim, vague
clever ignorant, stupid, foolish, untalented
climb descend, go/come down
cloak reveal, disclose, unmask
close open, unfold, begin
clown 1. act/behave sensibly/wisely 2. sage
clumsy agile, graceful, careful, skillful
clutch release, let go, free, liberate
coarse 1. smooth, polished 2. polite, civil
coax discourage, dissuade, dishearten
coil uncoil, unwind, unwrap
cold 1. warm, hot 2. close, affectionate
collapse build, erect, construct
collect disperse, broadcast, scatter
collide separate, go apart, part
colossal small, tiny, miniature
combat peace, lull, truce
combine separate, split, divide
come leave, go, quit, depart
comfort 1. discomfort 2. discourage, dishearten
comic tragic, serious, dignified
command obey, follow, accept
commence finish, end, stop, conclude
commit 1. cease, fail 2. recall, receive
common uncommon, unusual, extraordinary
companion enemy, opponent, antagonist
company 1. individual 2. privacy
compare contrast, differ
compel prevent, preclude
compete help, assist, cooperate
competent incompetent, incapable, unskilled
complain praise, commend, approve
complete 1. initiate, begin 2. incomplete, partial
compliment criticize, blame, insult
compose 1. break up, scatter 2. disturb
conceal disclose, uncover, reveal, expose
conceit humility, humbleness, meekness, simplicity
concentrate 1. daydream 2. scatter, spread
concern calm, composure, unconcern
conclude begin, start, open, initiate
condemn praise, approve, commend, pardon
condense expand, lengthen, extend
conduct misconduct, mislead, misdirect
confess conceal, hide, cover up
confident uncertain, unsure, insecure
confidential open, revealed, disclosed
confine release, free, discharge
confuse 1. arrange, order 2. enlighten, inform
connect disconnect, unfasten, untie
conquer lose, fail, surrender, give in
consider disregard, ignore, scorn
considerable small, meager, insufficient
considerate unkind, selfish, spiteful
construct dismantle, pull down, destroy
consume 1. yield, create 2. collect, gather
content discontent, unhappiness, displeasure
contest peace, harmony, cooperation
continue discontinue, cease, conclude
contract expand, enlarge, extend, inflate
contradict agree with, allow, grant
control mismanage, misdirect, mislead
convenient inconvenient, unsuitable, inappropriate
cool 1. warm, hot 2. rash, emotional
core outside, outer part
correct incorrect, wrong, inaccurate
correspond disagree, differ, vary
costly cheap, inexpensive, low-priced
couple disunite, disconnect, uncouple
courage cowardice, fear, timidity
courtesy discourtesy, rudeness, impoliteness
cover uncover, reveal, disclose, expose
crafty honest, straightforward, frank, sincere
cram empty, discharge, remove, release
crazy sensible, reasonable, logical, sane
credit discredit, dishonor, disgrace
criminal innocent, virtuous, legal, lawful
crisp soft, tender, flabby
criticize praise, applaud, commend
cross 1. support, agree with 2. please, charm
crowd 1. individual, single, solitary 2. disperse
crude 1. refined, polished 2. genteel, courteous
cruel kind, gentle, considerate, compassionate
crust inside, interior, core, center, kernel, heart
cry laugh, grin, chuckle

cultivate 1. reap, gather, harvest 2. destroy, reject, lay waste
cunning honest, frank, open, sincere
curious 1. indifferent, uninterested 2. ordinary, normal
current out-of-date, old-fashioned, obsolete
curse bless, sanctify, praise, commend
customer seller, vendor, shopkeeper
daily rarely, infrequently, irregularly
dainty indelicate, inelegant, coarse
damage repair, mend, fix, preserve, protect
damp 1. dry, arid 2. encourage
danger safety, security
dare play safe, accept, comply
daring shy, timid, afraid, cowardly
dark bright, light, vivid, clear, sunny, cheerful
dart dawdle, linger, loiter
dash 1. loiter, linger, dawdle
dawn 1. nightfall, sunset 2. end, finish
day night, night-time
dead alive, living, alert, sensitive
deaden increase awareness/vitality, amplify
deadly healthy, life-giving, stimulating
deaf 1. able to hear 2. attentive, mindful
deal collect, gather, hoard, store
dear cheap, inexpensive, low-priced
debate agree, concur, cooperate
debt credit, gain, benefit
deceive be honest/truthful/straight, undeceive
decent indecent, improper, vulgar, unseemly
decide delay, postpone, unsettle
declare conceal, hide, cover up, disguise
decline 1. accept 2. increase, rise, improve
decorate deface, disfigure, mar, spoil
decrease increase, enlarge, expand
defeat 1. surrender, submit 2. victory, conquest
defect improvement, advantage
defend 1. desert, leave, abandon 2. attack, assault
definite uncertain, indistinct, indefinite
deformed shapely, graceful, elegant
defraud reward, pay, recompense
delay advance, accelerate, hasten, hurry
deliberate unintentional, impetuous, hasty
delicate 1. strong, tough 2. uncouth, coarse
delicious bitter, nasty, unpalatable, unsavory
delight displease, sadden, disappoint
deliver keep back, retain, return
demand give, hand over, offer, present
demolish construct, erect, build, restore
dense 1. thin, scanty, sparse 2. intelligent
deny admit, allow, accept, grant
depart remain, wait, stay, return
depression 1. mound, hillock 2. happiness
derelict occupied, well-kept
descend go/get up, rise, mount, ascend
descent rise, ascent, climb
desert 1. occupy, inhabit 2. fertile, fruitful
deserve be unworthy/undeserving of
desirable undesirable, unwanted, unattractive
desire reject, dislike, disregard
despair hope, encouragement, optimism
desperate 1. calm, composed 2. hopeful, confident
despise like, love, approve of, commend
destroy make, build, create, renew
detach attach, fasten, tie, join, unite
detain release, set free, liberate, deliver
detect not notice, pass over/by, miss
determined irresolute, undecided, undetermined
detest like, love, cherish, care for
develop contract, condense, shorten, reduce
devoted disloyal, unfaithful, inconstant, indifferent
dictate follow orders, ask, beg, beseech, pray
die live, survive, flourish
different similar, alike, the same
difficulty help, assistance, ease, comfort
dignity humility, simplicity, informality
diligent lazy, idle, careless, slothful
dim bright, clear, conspicuous
din quiet, silence, calm, tranquillity
dingy clean, bright, unfaded
dip mound, hill, rise, upwards slope
direct indirect, round-about, circuitous
dirt cleanliness, tidiness
disaster blessing, benefit, boon
discipline indiscipline, disorder, unruliness
disgrace honor, favor, praise
disguise reveal, uncover, unmask, unveil

disgusting agreeable, pleasing, charming
dismal bright, cheerful, gay, pleasant
dismiss employ, engage, admit, assemble
displace arrange, order, adjust, group
display hide, cover, conceal, camouflage
displease please, charm, beguile, amuse
distant 1. near, close 2. friendly, sociable
distinct 1. indistinct, vague 2. connected
distress pleasure, gladness, comfort
distribute collect, gather, keep, store
distrust trust, confidence, faith, belief
disturb calm, quiet, soothe, appease
divide join, unite, combine, mix, bind
dodge meet, approach, confront
donate receive, take, retain, accept
doubtful certain, sure, definite, decided
drab bright, exciting, vivid, cheerful
drag push, shove, thrust
drain fill, replenish
drastic mild, moderate, feeble
draw push, shove, thrust
dreadful pleasing, pleasant, harmless, innocuous
dreary bright, cheerful, exciting, pleasing
dress undress, disrobe
drive discourage, dissuade, restrain
drop lift, raise, ascend, elevate
drown increase, amplify, intensify
drowsy wide-awake, alert
dry wet, damp, moist, soaked, humid
dual 1. single 2. manifold
due undeserved, unsuitable, inappropriate
dull 1. interesting 2. bright 3. intelligent 4. keen
duty pleasure, leisure, irresponsibility
dwell leave, quit, vacate, abandon
dwindle increase, enlarge, multiply
dye leave natural color, bleach
each all
eager indifferent, uninterested, shy
early 1. recent, present 2. late, behind
earn lose, forfeit, give up
ease 1. discomfort, trouble 2. aggravate, increase
easy difficult, hard, involved
eccentric normal, ordinary, sensible
edge center, middle
effect 1. cause, origin 2. neglect, overlook
effective 1. incapable, incompetent 2. unimpressive
efficient incompetent, ineffective
effort ease, rest, relaxation
elaborate 1. plain, simple 2. simplify
elapse stand/remain still
elastic inelastic, inflexible, rigid, stiff
elated sad, gloomy, miserable
elect dismiss, reject, disregard, ignore
elegant awkward, ungainly, inelegant
elementary advanced, difficult, complex
eliminate keep, retain, maintain, preserve
eloquent uncommunicative, unimpressive, inarticulate
embark disembark, return
embarrass assure, comfort
embrace 1. unclasp 2. exclude
emerge submerge, retreat, hide
emergency 1. routine, regular, normal 2. security
eminent unknown, obscure, nondescript
employ dismiss, sack, discharge, fire
empty 1. fill, replenish 2. full, occupied
enchant disenchant, displease, offend
encounter avoid, evade, dodge
encourage discourage, dishearten
end begin, start, commence, open, cause
endanger make safe/secure
endless brief, short, limited
endure give in, yield, surrender
enemy friend, ally, companion
energetic inactive, lethargic, lazy
engage 1. dismiss, discharge 2. withdraw
enjoyment sadness, misery, unhappiness
enlarge diminish, decrease, reduce
enlighten 1. darken 2. baffle, confuse
enormous little, small, tiny, miniature
enough insufficient, inadequate, poor
enrage placate, pacify, please, charm
enter go out, quit, depart from, vacate
entertain bore, weary, irritate
enthusiasm unconcern, indifference
entice repel, reject, disregard, ignore
entire partial, incomplete, fragmentary
entrance exit, way out, retreat

envy tolerance, acceptance, goodwill
equal unequal, different, differing
equivalent not alike, dissimilar, unequal
erase keep, retain, restore
erect 1. lower, take apart 2. horizontal, flat
error correction, amendment
escape 1. remain, stay 2. meet, confront
escort disregard, mislead, misguide
essential inessential, dispensable, unimportant
establish disestablish, dissolve, destroy
eternal brief, short, limited
evade meet, encounter, confront
evaporate materialize, appear
even uneven, odd, inexact, irregular
eventually firstly, immediately, directly
everlasting brief, short, limited
evident obscure, indistinct, concealed
evil virtue, goodness, justice
exact inexact, inaccurate, incorrect
exaggerate understate, be realistic
examine ignore, disregard, avoid
exasperate please, soothe, satisfy
exceed fall/go below/behind
excel fail, lose, falter, be inferior
excellent poor, inferior, bad
exceptional unexceptional, ordinary
excess shortage, lack, deficiency
excite calm, quiet, soothe, pacify
exclude include, leave/keep in
excuse accuse, blame, condemn
exertion inactivity, rest, relaxation
exhaust 1. refresh, invigorate 2. replenish
exhibit conceal, cover, hide
exist die out, pass away, fade, wither, perish
exit entrance, way in, inlet
expend decrease, contract, deflate
expel admit, enter, absorb, take in
expense profit, gain, income
expensive cheap, inexpensive, low-priced
experience inexperience, ignorance
expert 1. inexpert, unskilled 2. amateur, beginner, novice
expose conceal, hide, cover
express suppress, withhold, conceal
exquisite unattractive, ugly, displeasing
extend 1. shorten, contract 2. receive, take
exterior interior, inside, internal, inner
exterminate protect, preserve, conserve
external interior, inside, internal, inner
extract return, push/pull/put back
extraordinary ordinary, common, usual, unimportant
extravagance thrift, economy, care
fabulous 1. factual, authentic 2. simple, ordinary, commonplace
fade grow, flourish, revive, increase
fail 1. pass, succeed 2. improve, flourish
faint 1. clear, distinct 2. strong, vigorous
fair 1. unfair, unjust 2. ugly, unattractive 3. dull, inclement 4. unsatisfactory, not acceptable
faithful disloyal, inconstant, unreliable
fake real, true, genuine, authentic, original
fall 1. rise, ascend 2. increase, appreciate
false 1. real, genuine 2. correct, right 3. loyal, faithful, trustworthy
familiar 1. unknown, uncommon, rare 2. formal, distant, unfriendly
famous unknown, obscure, unimportant, nondescript
fancy 1. fact, reality, truth 2. plain, simple, not decorative
far near, close, adjacent, handy
farther nearer, closer
fascinate repel, displease, disenchant
fast 1. slow, sluggish, lethargic 2. loose, insecure 3. feed, feast, eat
fasten detach, untie, disconnect, uncouple
fat thin, lean, slim, skinny
fatal harmless, safe, innocuous
fatigue revive, strengthen, enliven, exhilarate, invigorate 2. freshness, vigor
favorable unfriendly, unhelpful, unkind, not well-disposed, unfavorable
fear courage, bravery, boldness, confidence
feeble strong, powerful, robust, firm
feminine masculine, male, manly
ferocious meek, timid, gentle, tame, docile
fetch return, take/send back
fierce meek, timid, gentle, tame, mild
fill empty, drain, deplete, exhaust, vacate
final first, opening, initial, primary

find lose, mislay, waste
fine 1. coarse, crude, poor 2. dull, wet, inclement 3. reward, payment, bonus
finish begin, commence, start, open, initiate
fit unfit, unsuitable, inappropriate
fix 1. detach, disconnect 2. damage, ruin 3. unsettle, cancel
flat 1. uneven, perpendicular, hilly 2. lively, vivacious
flee return, come/go back, remain, stay
flexible inflexible, rigid, unbending, implacable
fling catch, grab, clutch, clasp, hold
float sink, settle, descend, alight
flourish do badly, wither, fade, wane, decline
foe friend, ally, companion, comrade
foggy clear, plain, distinct
follow 1. lead, guide, direct 2. ignore, disregard 3. misunderstand, not comprehend 4. precede, go before
fool 1. sage, genius, expert 2. be serious/honest
foolhardy prudent, thoughtful, cautious, careful
forbid allow, permit, tolerate
force 1. discourage, restrain 2. weakness, delicacy, gentleness
foreign familiar, known, native
forget remember, recall, recollect
forgive blame, accuse, charge, condemn
forlorn happy, contented, satisfied
former latter, following, succeeding
forsake keep, retain, maintain, own
fortunate unfortunate, unlucky, ill-fated
fortune 1. certainty 2. poverty
foul 1. fair, tasteful, pleasant 2. clean, pure
fraction whole, full amount, total
fragile strong, sturdy, robust, firm
frantic calm, composed, undisturbed, nonchalant
free 1. capture, seize, imprison, arrest 2. ungenerous, illiberal 3. restrained
frequent rare, uncommon, infrequent, few
friendly unfriendly, hostile, antagonistic
frighten calm, soothe, comfort, pacify
front back, rear, posterior
fruitful infertile, barren, unprofitable
full 1. empty, vacant 2. incomplete, partial
funny serious, grave, sober, dignified
furious calm, composed, gentle, placid
futile effective, profitable, worthwhile
gain 1. lose, mislay 2. decrease, reduce
gallant timid, afraid, frightened, cowardly
game 1. work, employment 2. hunter, predator 3. timid, cowardly 4. agile, uninjured
gather scatter, distribute, disperse
gaudy dull, dark, drab, dreary
gaunt plump, fat, fleshy, flabby
gay serious, gloomy, mournful, depressed
gaze glance, glimpse
general unusual, uncommon, rare, irregular
generous 1. illiberal, mean, miserly 2. insufficient, inadequate
genial ungenial, unsociable
gentle 1. harsh, rough, unkind, brutal 2. dishonorable, not genteel, vulgar
genuine false, sham, fake, counterfeit, unsound, insincere, dishonest
get lose, return, reject, give back
ghastly pleasing, charming, attractive
giant small, tiny, miniature, minute, dwarf
giddy 1. steady, stable, sober 2. constant, reliable
gigantic small, tiny, miniature, minute
give receive, take, accept, return
glad 1. sad, displeased, unhappy 2. dull, ugly, dreary, cheerless
glamorous ugly, unattractive, plain, simple
glance gaze, watch, stare
glare 1. dullness, dimness 2. smile, grin
glimpse gaze, watch, stare
gloomy happy, joyful, gay, cheerful
glorious shameful, unworthy, dishonorable
glossy dull, dim, unpolished, lusterless
glum happy, joyful, gay, cheerful
glutton abstemious eater/person
go 1. come, return 2. stand/remain still 3. be out of action/inactive/motionless
good 1. untrue, improper, unjust, immoral, bad, corrupt, unsatisfactory, inadequate, poor, ungenerous 2. unfavorable, unprofitable, unhelpful, inefficient, adulterated, tainted, inferior 3. unskilled, untalented, stupid
gorgeous simple, plain, dull, drab, dreary
govern 1. misgovern, mismanage 2. obey, follow
grab return, give back, fling, throw
graceful ungraceful, inelegant, unattractive
gracious discourteous, unmannerly, disagreeable

gradual fast, quick, rapid, sudden, abrupt
grand poor, inferior, ordinary, commonplace
grant 1. take, receive 2. disallow, prohibit, refuse
grasp 1. release, let go 2. misunderstand, not comprehend
grateful ungrateful, unthankful, unacceptable
great small, little, poor, inferior, ordinary, commonplace, unimportant, insignificant, unknown, undistinguished
greedy generous, liberal, openhanded
greet ignore, disregard, not acknowledge
grief 1. happiness, joy, contentment 2. good fortune
grip release, unclasp, let go, free
groan laugh, praise, applaud, commend
gross 1. small, little, lean, thin 2. refined, clean, delicate 3. indistinct, concealed, hidden 4. net, after deductions
ground 1. sky, heavens 2. top, roof
grow wither, fade, decrease, shrink, contract
grown-up childish, puerile, youthful, immature
gruesome pleasant, pleasing, attractive, elegant
grumble commend, praise, applaud
guess know, be certain/sure/confident
guide 1. misguide, mislead, misdirect 2. follow, obey
guile honesty, truthfulness, frankness, candor
gullible shrewd, astute, discerning
habitual rare, seldom, irregular, infrequent
haggard fresh, lively, energetic, untroubled
hail ignore, disregard, avoid
halt start, begin, commence, go, advance, proceed
hamper encourage, aid, help, assist, support
handicap advantage, help, aid, assistance, benefit
handsome ugly, unattractive, ungraceful
handy useless, inconvenient, awkward, clumsy, remote
haphazard orderly, settled, planned, organized
happy sad, miserable, dejected, unhappy
harass aid, help, support, soothe, please
hard 1. soft, yielding 2. sympathetic, kind 3. easy, not difficult
hardship good fortune, pleasure, benefit
hardy weak, feeble, frail, fragile, delicate
harm help, assist, benefit, please, improve
harmless harmful, hurtful, damaging, injurious
harsh 1. easy, kind, sensitive 2. soft, pleasant, agreeable
harvest sow, set, broadcast, scatter
hasty 1. slow, unhurried 2. careful, considerate
hate like, love, admire, adore, cherish
hateful pleasing, pleasant, likeable, lovable, amiable
haughty humble, unassuming, simple, shy
haul push, shove, thrust, drive
have 1. disown 2, give up, relinquish, repudiate, reject, forfeit 3. refuse to allow/permit
hazard 1. safety, safeguard 2. certainty, guarantee
hazy clear, plain, distinct, bright
headlong 1. feet first/foremost 2. carefully, thoughtfully
headstrong careful, cautious, prudent, irresolute
heal damage, injure, harm, hurt
healthy unhealthy, ailing, infirm, sickly, unsound, unwholesome
heap scatter, spread, disperse, broadcast
heart exterior, outside, crust
heartless feeling, gentle, kind, sympathetic
hearty 1. unfriendly, unsociable 2. insincere, hypocritical 3. weak, delicate
heat 1. cold, coldness, coolness 2. calmness, composure 3. unconcern, indifference
heavy 1. light, slight, small, trivial, yielding 2. bright, optimistic, hopeful
hectic calm, peaceful, uneventful
hedge meet, face, confront, be decisive
heed ignore, disregard, avoid, disobey
hefty light, small, slight, weak, feeble
help hinder, hamper, obstruct, impede
herald ignore, conceal, usher out
heroic unheroic, cowardly, scared
hesitate hurry, hasten, proceed
hide uncover, reveal, expose, disclose
hideous beautiful, fair, handsome, attractive
high 1. low 2. unimportant, nondescript 3. low-pitched, weak
hilarious unhappy, sad, gloomy, depressing
hill vale, dale, valley, hollow, depression
hinder help, aid, assist, support
hindmost first, foremost

hire dismiss, discharge
hitch 1. unfasten, untie 2. help, solution
hoard spread, distribute, scatter, spend
hold 1. release, free 2. reject, lose, forfeit 3. disbelieve, deny
holiday work, employment, job
hollow 1. solid, full 2. sincere, frank, unpretentious 3. mound, hill
holy unholy, sacrilegious, defiled, profane
homely comely, attractive, pretentious, sophisticated
honest dishonest, untruthful, deceitful
honor dishonor, disgrace, shame, disrepute
hoodwink enlighten, undeceive, inform
hope be resigned, be pessimistic about, despair
hopeless hopeful, promising, optimistic
horrible pleasing, pleasant, attractive, charming
horrid pleasing, attractive, agreeable
horrify calm, soothe, please, charm, captivate
hospitable unfriendly, unsociable, unneighborly
host 1. few, small number/quantity 2. customer, guest
hostile friendly, amicable, hospitable
hot 1. cold, frigid, icy 2. indifferent, slow
huge small, tiny, miniature, minute, microscopic
human inhuman, brutal, cruel, pitiless
humane inhumane, brutal, cruel, without pity/mercy
humble proud, vain, arrogant, haughty
humor 1. tragedy, seriousness 2. disagree with
hungry well-fed, replete, full
hunt escape, flee, fly
hurl catch, grab, clutch, clasp, seize, hold
hurry slow down, go slow, falter
hurt heal, cure, aid, assist, protect, preserve
hypocritical sincere, honest, frank, candid, straightforward
icy 1. warm, hot, heated 2. friendly, sociable
ideal imperfect, unsatisfactory'
identical different, unlike, dissimilar, unequal
idiotic sensible, sound, reasonable, rational
idle active, busy, occupied, engaged
ignite extinguish, put out, snuff
ignorant knowledgeable, educated, well-informed
ignore notice, observe, heed
ill 1. well, fit, healthy 2. good, lucky, fortunate
illegal legal, lawful, permissible, allowed
illness health, vigor, fitness
illogical logical, reasonable, sensible, rational
illuminate darken, shade
illusion reality, fact, truth, actuality
imaginary real, factual, not abstract
immediately soon, shortly, presently, later
immense small, little, tiny, minute
immerse emerge, draw/pull out
immortal mortal, impermanent, transient
immovable 1. movable, mobile, portable 2. irresolute, wavering
impart withold, suppress, conceal
impartial partial, biased, unfair, prejudiced
impatient patient, calm, composed
impede impel, propel, help, assist
imperfect perfect, complete, flawless, unblemished
impertinent polite, courteous, respectful
impetuous cautious, thoughtful, mindful, prudent
implore give, grant, allow, permit
impolite polite, courteous, civil, mannerly
important unimportant, trivial, unnecessary
impose take off, remove, abolish
imposing unimposing, unimpressive, ordinary, commonplace
impressive unimpressive, ordinary, insignificant
impromptu prepared, planned, rehearsed
improper proper, correct, becoming, suitable
improve worsen, become inferior, deteriorate
imprudent prudent, wise, cautious, thoughtful
impudent polite, courteous, respectful
impulsive careful, cautious, restrained, prudent
impure pure, unadulterated, clean
inadequate adequate, suitable, sufficient
inappropriate appropriate, suitable, fitting
incessant irregular, intermittent, periodic
incompetent competent, capable, proficient
incorrect correct, right. accurate, exact
increase decrease, lessen, reduce, fall
incredible credible, acceptable, easy to believe
indecent decent, proper, correct, seemly
indefinite definite, certain, sure

independent dependent, obedient, subordinate
indifferent interested, concerned, bothered
indirect direct, straight, nearest
indispensable inessential, unneccessary, not required/needed
indistinct distinct, clear, plain, definite, certain
industrious idle, lazy, inactive, unoccupied
ineffective effective, useful, appropriate
inevitable doubtful, uncertain, unsure
inferior 1. above, on top, elevated 2. superior, first class, better
infinite finite, limited, definite
infirm 1. firm, stable 2. strong, well, healthy
inflame extinguish, put out
inflate deflate, contract, shrink, decrease
inform not divulge, conceal, hide, learn
infrequent frequent, numerous, regular
infuriate calm, soothe, placate, mollify
ingenious foolish, untalented, simple
inhabit desert, vacate, abandon, forsake
inhuman human, humane, kind, compassionate
injure protect, preserve, help, assist
innocent guilty, blameworthy, condemned
inquire reply, retort, answer
inquisitive incurious, indifferent
insecure secure, safe, guarded, protected
insignificant significant, important, consequential
insolent polite, courteous, respectful
instant delayed, slow, tardy, belated
instruct learn, obey, follow
insufficient sufficient, adequate, enough
insult compliment, commend, praise
intact damaged, injured, broken, defective
intelligent stupid, dull, backward, retarded
intentional accidental, unprepared, unplanned
intricate simple, easy, uncomplicated
invalid 1. valid, acceptable, applicable 2. fit/healthy person
irate calm, pleased, contented, serene
irksome easy, pleasant, agreeable, interesting
irritable calm, placid, unruffled, serene
irritate calm, soothe, please, pacify
jagged smooth, even, level
jam release, free, liberate, unpack
jealous content, trusting, loyal, tolerant
jeer applaud, praise, compliment, commend
jerk push, shove, thrust, poke, jab
jittery calm, relaxed, composed, confident
join disunite, untie, detach, disconnect
jolly sad, solemn, serious, gloomy, surly
joy unhappiness, sadness, misery, gloom
jubilant unhappy, sad, miserable, downcast
jumble order, put in order, arrange, sort out
just unjust, unfair, partial, biased, improper, unrighteous, unbecoming
justice unfairness, partiality, bad treatment
juvenile adult, grown-up, mature person
keen 1. uninterested, indifferent, inactive, unenthusiastic 2. dull, obtuse, insensitive
keep throw away, discard, disobey, ignore
kill spare, protect, safeguard, preserve
kin strangers, foreigners, aliens
kind unkind, mean, spiteful, harsh, cruel
know misunderstand, not comprehend/realize, be unversed in/ignorant/unaware
knowing uninformed, ignorant, unaware
knowledge ignorance, lack/shortage of information
labor ease, comfort, leisure, pleasure
laborious easy, simple, light, lazy
lack abundance, adequacy, wealth
lag hasten, hurry, accelerate
lame 1. uninjured, whole 2. satisfactory, adequate, acceptable
land embark, board, go aboard
large small, little, tiny, wee, minute, miniature
last 1. first, foremost, primary, initial, opening 2. fade away, disappear
lasting temporary, transient, short-lived
late 1. early, prompt, immediate 2. present, living, existing
laugh cry, weep, sob
laughable sad, sorrowful, serious, solemn
lavish plain, simple, poor, cheap, inexpensive
lawful unlawful, illegal, illicit, illegitimate
lawless law-abiding, orderly, well-conducted
lax strict, rigid, firm, reliable
lazy active, busy, industrious, diligent
lead 1. mislead, misguide 2. follow, support
leader follower, supporter, adherent

lean 1. straighten up, become erect 2. fat, stout, plump, obese
learned ignorant, uneducated, illiterate
learning ignorance, illiteracy
leave 1. return, enter 2. prohibition, ban 3. work, employment
left right, right-hand, right-hand side
legal illegal, unlawful, illicit, illegitimate
legend fact, truth, actuality, history
legendary factual, true, actual, historical
legitimate 1. illegitimate, unlawful, illicit, unlawful 2. false, pretended, counterfeit
leisure work, job, employment
lengthen shorten, decrease, reduce, contract
lenient strict, rigid, firm, severe
lessen increase, extend, expand
let prevent, prohibit, ban
level 1. perpendicular, inclined, uneven, irregular 2. erect, build
liberate arrest, seize, hold, detain
lie 1. stand, sit 2. tell the truth, be honest
lift 1. lower 2. hindrance, obstruction
light 1. dark, dull, shady, unlit, unilluminated 2. strong, robust, heavy, weighty
lighten 1. darken, shade 2. increase, enlarge, make greater
like 1. dislike, disapprove of, detest, abhor 2. not alike, dissimilar, unlike
limit increase, extend, raise, allow, encourage
limp stiff, rigid, firm, erect
linger hurry, hasten, be quick/swift
link disconnect, uncouple, unfasten
list straighten up, become erect
listen ignore, disregard, not attend
listless active, energetic, vigorous
little large, big, great, huge, enormous
live 1. die 2, inactive, slow 3. extinguished, harmless, dead
lively 1. inactive, slow, sluggish, lethargic 2. sad, gloomy, melancholy, unhappy
loathe like, love, adore, admire, cherish
lofty 1. low 2. humble, simple
loiter hurry, hasten, be quick/swift
lonely crowded, accompanied
long short, brief, abrupt, immediate
look ignore, disregard
lose find, discover, retrieve
lot few, several, not much/many
loud quiet, silent, soft, faint, subdued
love dislike, loathe, hate, abhor
lovely plain, simple, ugly, unattractive, displeasing
loyalty disloyalty, infidelity, inconstancy
lucky unlucky, unfortunate, ill-fated
lull irritate, aggravate, anger, excite, stimulate
lustrous dim, dull, dark, unpolished
luxuriant meager, sparse, slight, poor
luxury need, want, poverty
macabre pleasing, beautiful, lovely, charming
mad 1. sane, sensible, rational 2. calm, composed
magnificent ordinary, commonplace, insignificant
magnify reduce, minimize
maid matron, married woman
maim preserve, guard, protect, spare
main lesser, less important, secondary
maintain 1. abandon, desert, disown 2. deny, disclaim
majestic undignified, ordinary, common, meek, plebeian
major minor, lesser, smaller, inferior, junior
majority minority, lesser/smaller part
make 1. unmake, destroy 2. discourage, dissuade
malady 1. remedy, cure 2. good health
male female, feminine, womanly, ladylike
mammoth small, little, tiny, miniature, minute
man female, woman, lady
manage mismanage, misdirect, disorganize
manageable unruly, undisciplined, wild, untamed
manhood childhood, youth
mankind womankind
manly feminine, womanly, ladylike
manners misconduct, discourtesy, incivility
manual mechanical, by machine
manufacture dismantle, destroy
many few, several, rare, infrequent
margin center, middle, midpoint
marine land, terrestrial
mark 1. clean, renovate, clear 2. ignore, disregard

maroon rescue, save, deliver
marry divorce, untie, disunite
marvelous ordinary, commonplace, unimpressive
masculine feminine, female, womanly, ladylike
mask reveal, disclose, expose, uncover
mass small quantity/amount, shortage, scarcity, paucity
massacre preserve, protect, spare
master 1. slave, servant 2. pupil, scholar, student 3. surrender, yield, give in
mastery inferiority, slavery, bondage
match 1. be dissimilar, disagree 2. inferior
material unreal, unsubstantial, irrelevant, abstract
matt smooth, flat, shiny
matter be irrelevant/unimportant/insignificant
mature unripe, young, immature
maximum minimum, smallest, least, lowest
maybe certainly, definitely, positively
meager ample, abundant, plentiful, copious
mean 1. ample, abundant, plentiful, sufficient 2. refined, kind, generous
meaning nonsense, unimportance, insignificance
meaningless purposeful, sensible, rational, logical, significant, meaningful
meddle ignore, avoid, disregard
meek harsh, arrogant, haughty, majestic
meet 1. avoid 2. dismiss, disperse 3. fail
melancholy happiness, joy, gladness, merriment
mellow unripe, immature, imperfect
member non-member, outsider
memorize forget, put aside
menace protect, preserve, help, support
mend break, damage, deteriorate
mention conceal, hide, ignore, disregard
mercy harshness, cruelty, brutality
merge separate, divide, come/go apart, disunite
merry unhappy, melancholy, cheerless, dreary
mess order, neatness, tidiness
method disorder, disorderliness, untidiness
methodical disorderly, unsystematic, without purpose
middle outside, exterior
might weakness, gentleness, meekness
mild 1. severe, harsh, unkind 2. cold, stormy
military 1. civilian, civil 2. naval
mind 1. neglect, disregard, ignore 2. forget 3. approve of, commend
mindful unmindful, inattentive, unheedful
miniature big, large, huge, enormous
minimum maximum, most, largest, highest
minor major, larger, greater, senior, superior
minority majority, greater/larger part
minus plus, with, additional to, positive
minute very/extremely big/large, enormous
miraculous ordinary, usual, commonplace
mirth sadness, melancholy, gloominess, unhappiness, misery
mischief 1. good conduct/behavior 2. protection, care
misconduct good conduct/behavior, order
miserable happy, gay, jolly, glad, gleeful
misfortune good fortune/luck, success
miss 1. notice, observe, hit 2. mistress, Mrs.
mix separate, segregate, part
mobile immobile, inactive, immovable, not portable
mock 1. real, genuine, actual 2. cheer, applaud, praise, commend, approve
model unmake, misshape, deform
moderate 1. unreasonable, extreme, fanatical 2. increase
modern old, ancient, old-fashioned, out-of-date, obsolescent
modest bold, extravagant, vain, conceited
moist dry, arid, dehydrated
molest comfort, console, protect, defend, help, assist
moment 1. age, long time, eternity 2. unimportance, insignificance
monarch subject, follower, subordinate
monotonous irregular, interesting, exciting
monster tame animal, kind/kindly/humane person
moody calm, composed, unruffled, phlegmatic
mope be content/cheerful/spirited
moral immoral, bad, unethical, dishonorable, dishonest, disgraceful, disgusting
motion inaction, inactivity, immobility
motionless active, moving, shifting, mobile, not still/stationary

mount 1. go/come/climb down, descend 2. hollow, valley, depression

mourn rejoice, exult

move 1. leave untouched 2. return 3. remain, halt, pause, stand still

multiply decrease, reduce, diminish, lessen

murder preserve, protect, spare

musty new, fresh

mutiny obey, serve, follow

mystery solution, answer, evidence

nag praise, applaud, commend, soothe

naked clothed, covered, dressed

narrow 1. wide, broad, thick, spacious, unlimited 2. impartial, broadminded

nasty pleasant, nice, agreeable, inoffensive, clean, unpolluted

native unnatural, civilized

natural affected, sophisticated, pretentious, abnormal, unusual

naughty good, well-behaved, polite, obedient, dutiful

near 1. far, distant 2. unrelated, disconnected

neat 1. untidy, unclean, slovenly 2. unskillful 3. impure, adulterated

necessary unnecessary, inessential

need 1. plenty, abundance, luxury 2. own, hold, possess

needy rich, prosperous, wealthy, affluent

negative positive, definite, correct

neglect care for, maintain, look after, preserve, remember

neglectful careful, thoughtful, considerate, attentive

nerve fear, cowardice, apprehension

nervous calm, composed, tranquil, bold, brave, resolute

net 1. release, free, liberate 2. gross

neutral partial, biased, prejudiced

new 1. old, out-of-date, obsolescent, familiar, previously known 2. previous, earlier

next 1. preceding, previous, prior, recent 2. at a distance, away from

nice 1. nasty, unpleasant, unfavorable, bad, disagreeable, unfriendly, ugly 2. inexact, inaccurate

nimble awkward, ungainly, slow, lethargic, dull

noble 1. ignoble, unworthy, dishonorable, mean, undignified, inferior 2. peasant, serf

nobody 1. somebody, someone, some person 2. person of importance/consequence

noise quiet, peace, stillness, silence

none some, someone, somebody, something

nonsense sense, logic, reason, sanity, wisdom

normal abnormal, irregular, unnatural, unusual,

notable undistinguished, obscure, unknown, unimportant

note 1. insignificant, unimportant 2. ignore, overlook, disregard, miss, not observe

notice ignore, disregard, miss

nourish starve, deprive, feed inadequately

novel old, out-of-date, unoriginal, common, ordinary, mediocre

novice professional, expert, master, specialist

nude clothed, dressed, covered, unexposed

nuisance help, assistance, helpful/inoffensive person

numerous few, several, not many

nutritious unwholesome, weakening, injurious

obedient rebellious, unyielding, undisciplined, disorderly, unruly, defiant

obey disobey, disregard, ignore

object approve, agree, consent, allow

oblige disoblige, hinder, hamper, obstruct

obscure 1. bright, clear, plain, distinct 2. notable, famous, distinguished, celebrated

observant 1. inattentive, careless, incautious, unwary 2. disobedient, defiant

observe 1. miss, overlook, ignore 2. disobey, break, violate, defy

obstacle help, aid, encouragement

obstinate yielding, submissive, obedient

obstruct help, aid, assist, support

obtain lose, return, forfeit, give up, spend

obvious obscure, unapparent, uncertain, indefinite

occasional frequent, regular, common

occupy leave, quit, abandon, desert, forsake, evacuate

odd 1. even, regular, uniform 2. normal, usual

odious nice, pleasant, pleasing, agreeable, charming, inoffensive

offend please, charm, oblige, satisfy, help, assist

offensive pleasing, charming, obliging, helpful

offer 1. take accept 2. levy, tax, duty

official unofficial, unauthorized

old 1. new, recent, modern, current, up-to-date 2. young, youthful 3. original, novel, stylish
omit include, insert
onward backward, backwards, rearward, rearwards, behind, to the rear
open 1. shut, closed, covered, hidden, undisclosed 2. hypocritical, insincere 3. end, finish, conclude
opening 1. barrier, bar, barricade 2. ending, final, concluding, closing, last
opponent ally, friend, companion, mate, assistant
opportune inopportune, inconvenient, badly-timed
oppose help, assist, support, follow, obey
opposite same, alike, like, similar
opposition help, assistance, support, cooperation
optimistic pessimistic, unhopeful
order 1. obedience, acceptance 2. disorder, untidiness, disarray
orderly 1. disordered, chaotic, untidy 2. unruly, rebellious, disobedient
ordinary unusual, uncommon, odd, queer, strange, extraordinary
origin end, finish, result
originate end, finish, terminate, demolish, destroy
outlet inlet, entrance, way in, access
outside 1. inward, inwards, within 2. interior, internal, inside
outstanding inferior, unexceptional, obscure, ordinary, usual, commonplace
outward 1. inward, inwards, within 2. internal, on the inside
over 1. under, below, beneath 2. less/fewer than 3. begun, started, commenced, opened
overcome submit, surrender, yield, give in
overlook notice, note, heed, mind
overpower submit, surrender, yield, give in
overthrow be overthrown/abased, surrender
overwhelm submit, surrender, yield, give way
owe be in credit/a creditor
own 1. give up, hand over, forsake, abandon 2. deny, disclaim, dispute
pagan enlightened, believer
pain pleasure, enjoyment, contentment, tranquillity, peace
pair disunite, uncouple, untie
pale bright, brilliant, radiant, vivid, intense
paltry important, significant, worthwhile, essential
pamper punish, chastise, discipline, deny, deprive
pandemonium order, calm, tranquillity, peace, quiet, silence
panic calm, composure, peace, courage, order
parade dismiss, disperse
parched wet, moist, damp, soaked, sodden, humid
pardon 1. blame, accuse 2. punish, penalize
part 1. whole, total 2. join, unite 3. return
particular 1. indistinct, not exclusive, inessential 2. incautious, careless, not fastidious
partner opponent, competitor, rival, enemy
pass 1. follow, succeed, chase 2. receive, take 3. disallow, forbid, prohibit, ban 4. barrier
passion calm, composure, tranquillity, indifference, nonchalance
pastime work, employment, business
patient impatient, incautious, hasty, rash, impetuous, intolerant
pause continue, carry on, proceed, advance
pay 1. charge, levy 2. receive, accept
peaceful noisy, clamorous, tumultuous, frenzied, chaotic
peak bottom, base, lowest part, foundation
peculiar normal, usual, ordinary, commonplace
penalty prize, reward, gift, present
perfect imperfect, incomplete, defective, faulty, blemished, inglorious, not absolute
peril 1. safety, security 2. caution, care
perish 1. survive, live, exist, endure 2. keep fresh
permanent impermanent, transient, temporary, brief
permit prohibit, disallow, forbid, ban, bar, deny, refuse, prevent
perpendicular flat, level, horizontal
perpetual impermanent, transient, temporary, brief
perplex assure, convince, enlighten, instruct
persecute please, charm, encourage, support, assist
persevere 1. give in, yield, hesitate 2. cease, stop
persist 1. give in, yield, hesitate 2. cease, stop
personal 1. not private 2. public, impersonal
persuade discourage, dissuade, deter
pest 1. help, assistance 2. helpful/harmless/ inoffensive person

pet 1. wild animal 2. tease, pester, annoy, irritate
petty 1. important, significant, essential, great urgent, worthwhile 2. generous, tolerant
pick 1. reject, refuse, disallow 2. spread, scatter, disperse
piece total, whole, complete quantity/amount
pile disperse, broadcast, scatter, spread
pitiful cheerful, gay, contented, pleasing, attractive, charming
pity 1. indifference 2. cruelty, brutality, severity
place displace, move, transfer
plague help, assist, soothe, placate, pacify
plain 1. decorative, fine, grand, magnificent, sophisticated 2. obscure, complicated, indistinct 3. uneven, undulating
plan disarrange, unsettle, disorder
plant 1. uproot 2. displace, remove, pick/pull up
plants animals, fauna, animal-life
play work, employment, seriousness, solemnity
plead grant, allow, permit, concede
pleasant unpleasant, ugly, unattractive, disagreeable, drab
please displease, offend, irritate, bother, trouble, discomfort
plentiful scarce, sparse, meager, slender
pluck 1. return, put down 2. cowardice, timidity
plump thin, lean, slender, small, slight
plunge 1. emerge, come out 2. withdraw, pull back
polish make dull/lusterless
polite impolite, discourteous, uncivil, rude, bad-mannered, unmannerly
poor 1. rich, wealthy, prosperous, luxurious 2. fertile, fruitful 3. superior, superb
popular unpopular, unwanted, disliked
portable immobile, immovable, stationary, fixed
portion whole, all, full amount/quantity
positive negative, indefinite, uncertain, unsure
possess hand over, forsake, abandon, relinquish, give up
possibly certainly, decidedly, definitely
postpone 1. cancel 2. bring back/closer/nearer
poverty riches, wealth, prosperity, abundance, affluence
power weakness, feebleness, inability
practical 1. useless, pointless, futile, empty, ineffective 2. unskilled, unskillful, inefficient
praise blame, condemn, accuse, decry, deride, jeer
preceding following, succeeding, subsequent, later
precise inexact, inaccurate, incorrect, erratic, indefinite
prefer refuse, reject, decline
prejudice impartiality, fairness, tolerance
preliminary final, end, concluding
prepare disarrange, disarray, disorder
preposterous sensible, logical, reasonable, rational
presence absence, non-attendance
present 1. absent, not here, away 2. take, receive, accept 3. past 4. future
presently later, in the future
preserve 1. spoil, destroy 2. discard, dispose of
press 1. pull, tug 2. discourage, dissuade, deter
pressing unimportant, insignificant, trivial, trifling, not urgent
presume doubt, disbelieve, disregard, ignore
pretty plain, unattractive, ugly
prevent allow, permit, encourage, assist, help
previous following, succeeding, subsequent, later
priceless worthless, valueless, without value, cheap, inexpensive
prime 1. second, secondary, lesser, subordinate 2. second-rate, inferior, poor, imperfect 3. later life, old age
principal lesser, minor, small, less important, unimportant, trivial
prisoner escapee, fugitive
private 1. impersonal, public, open 2. busy, crowded, congested
prize 1. dislike, abhor, loathe 2. punishment, penalty, forfeiture, fine
probable improbable, unlikely, uncertain, doubtful, impossible
problem 1. solution, answer 2. help, aid
proceed 1. finish, end, halt 2. retreat, retire, withdraw
proclaim disclaim, deny, gainsay
produce 1. destroy, demolish, eradicate 2. return 3. accept
profit loss
progress 1. go back, retreat, return 2. stop, halt 3. decrease, fall, decline

prohibit allow, permit, tolerate, consent to, grant
prolong shorten, reduce, lessen, decrease, limit
prominent obscure, unknown, unimportant, not famous/celebrated, unseen, insignificant, commonplace
promise refusal, denial, non-acceptance, disagreement
promising not hopeful, gloomy, discouraging, pessimistic
prompt 1. slow, delayed, late, tardy, neglectful, unmindful 2. discourage, dissuade, deter, hinder, hamper
propel repel, drive back, return
proper improper, incorrect, inexact, inappropriate, unsuitable, unbecoming, unseemly
prosper fail, lose, do badly, decline
protect 1. neglect, disregard 2. attack, ill-treat, abuse
protest agree, consent, accept, allow, permit
proud 1. humble, simple, homely, modest, meek, unpretentious, respectful 2. undignified, ignoble
prove disprove, contradict, deny, gainsay
prudent imprudent, unwise, incautious, careless, rash, impetuous
public private, personal, confidential
pull push, shove, thrust, drive
punish 1. excuse, pardon, forgive, overlook 2. reward, recompense
pupil teacher, tutor, instructor, coach
purchase sell, vend, retail, peddle, dispose of
pure 1. impure, adulterated, unclean, tainted 2. blameworthy, imperfect, sullied, ignoble, without virtue, unchaste
purify make unclean, sully, dirty, spoil, soil, taint, adulterate
pursue escape, flee, fly, avoid, dodge
push 1. pull, tug, yank, draw 2. discourage, dissuade, deter, hinder, hamper
puzzle enlighten, inform, instruct
qualified unqualified, inept, incompetent, incapable, untrained
quarrel agree, understand
quarry hunter, pursuer, predator
quash support, uphold, follow, assist, help
queer 1. ordinary, normal, usual, regular, not suspect/suspicious/questionable 2. well, fit, not sick/faint/indisposed
quell uphold, support, encourage, assist
query answer, reply, retort, response
questionable unquestionable, certain, sure, definite, agreed, proven
quick 1. slow, sluggish, lethargic, slothful, inactive 2. dull, stupid, unintelligent 3. patient, careful, cautious, tolerant
quiet 1. noisy, audible, rowdy, clamorous, tumultuous, loud, excitable 2. active, obtrusive, garish, vivid
quit 1. return, go/come back, reoccupy 2. keep, retain, adopt 3. continue, carry on
quite incompletely, partially, partly
race slow down, linger, loiter, stroll
rack please, ease, relieve, alleviate
racket silence, quiet, calm, peace, serenity, tranquility
rage calm, composure, serenity
ragged neat, tidy, smart, elegant
raid 1. protect, defend 2. retreat, withdraw
rail praise, commend, applaud, approve
raise 1. drop, lower 2. decrease, lessen, diminish, reduce 3. neglect, abandon 4. disperse, spread 5. calm, soothe
ramble 1. stay, remain 2. keep to the subject
range stay, remain
rank 1. disarrange, disarray, separate 2. scanty, sparse 3. gentle, mild
rapid slow, sluggish, lethargic
rare frequent, common, usual, typical
rascal noble/fine/virtuous person, hero, saint
rash cautious, careful, thoughtful, prudent
rather 1. greatly, manifestly 2. less truly
rattle 1. quietness, silence 2. assure, encourage
ravenous well-fed, satisfied, satiated
raw 1. prepared, cooked 2. experienced, trained 3. painless, insensitive 4. warm, fine
reedy 1. unready, unwilling, unprepared 2. slow, hesitant, reluctant
real unreal, false, sham, bogus, counterfeit
realize misunderstand, not comprehend, be unaware
rear 1. front, fore part, anterior 2. first, foremost 3. neglect, fail to train/educate
reasonable unreasonable, improper, unjust, unfair
rebel 1. obey, follow, support, adhere 2. follower, supporter
recall 1. forget 2. send out

receive give, reject, lose, decline, refuse
recent 1. former, old 2. succeeding, following
reckless cautious, careful, thoughtful, prudent
recline sit up, stand
recognize misunderstand, miss
recollect forget, disregard
recommend disapprove of, condemn
recover 1. lose, mislay, drop 2. relapse, decline
recreation work, labor, employment
reduce 1. increase, enlarge 2. surrender, yield 3. strengthen
reflect overlook, ignore, disregard, neglect
refresh weaken, tire, exhaust
refuge trap, snare, pitfall, peril, danger
refuse accept, receive, take, acknowledge
regain lose, mislay, drop
regard 1. disregard, ignore 2. disrespect
regret rejoice, be glad/pleased/joyful
regular 1. irregular, impermanent 2. incorrect, improper, abnormal 3. erratic
reject accept, receive, take, get
relax 1. increase, tighten 2. strive, struggle, work
release l catch, capture, seize 2. keep, retain, hold
reliable unreliable, disloyal, unfaithful
relieve hinder, frustrate, distress, upset, agitate
reluctant willing, keen, eager, ardent
rely distrust, mistrust
remain go/get/come away, leave, depart, quit
remark ignore, disregard, overlook
remarkable simple, plain, common, ordinary, normal
remedy harm, hurt, damage
remember forget, overlook, miss, neglect
remote near, close, adjacent, neighboring
remove 1. replace, return 2. place, set down, plant
repair damage, destroy, break, fracture
replace remove, take away, displace
reply ask, demand, question, request
report suppress, withhold, conceal
rescue 1. lose, mislay, drop 2. capture, seize, imprison
reserve give up, lose, distribute, release
reserved 1. bold, sure, confident 2. released
resign retain, keep
resist submit, surrender, yield, give in
resolution indecision, hesitation
resourceful incompetent, inefficient, unimaginative
respect show disrespect, disregard, ignore
respectable dishonorable, indecent, not respected
responsible irresponsible, negligent, careless, thoughtless
restful uncomfortable, disturbed, unrelaxed
restless calm, peaceful, tranquil, placid
restore 1. remove, seize, take 2. damage, ruin, harm
restrain encourage, urge, persuade
restrict allow, permit, tolerate, sanction
result cause, origin, start, beginning
resume cease, end, finish, stop
retire 1. attack, advance, enter 2. arise, get up
retort ask, demand, question
return 1. take, obtain, get 2. retain, keep, hold 3. depart, go out, leave, quit
reveal conceal, cover, hide, mask
reverse 1. confirm, maintain 2. same side, obverse, face, front 3. victory, triumph, gain
revise ignore, disregard
revive 1. decline, relapse, deteriorate 2. die
revolt obey, follow, support, remain
revolting pleasing, attractive, charming
reward penalty, punishment, forfeiture
rich 1. poor, needy 2. infertile, barren 3. dull
riddle 1. answer, solution 2. manifestation
ridicule admire, praise, applaud, respect
ridiculous sensible, rational, reasonable, logical, proper, sound
right wrong, incorrect, improper, untrue, unfair, inappropriate
rigid loose, slack, lax, flexible, pliable, elastic
ripe unripe, immature, young
rise 1. sit, lie down, recline 2. descend, go downwards, fall, drop 3. decrease, lessen 4. end, finish 5. hollow, depression
risk security, safety, assurance
rival colleague, partner, ally, comrade
roam remain, rest, stay, stop
rob give, contribute, offer, return, replace
robust weak, feeble, frail, fragile, delicate
rogue upright/honest person, hero, saint
romantic unromantic, not fanciful, unimaginative

rot keep, preserve, conserve
rough 1. smooth, even, regular 2. calm, orderly 3. mild, gentle 4. polite, courteous, refined
round 1. square 2. straight, flat, level
rouse soothe, calm, placate, appease
routine irregular, unusual, exceptional, unofficial
row 1. agreement, conciliation 2. silence, quietness
rude polite, courteous, civil, respectful
ruin 1. restore, renew, refurbish 2. protect, improve
rumor factual/truthful/accurate story
run move/travel slowly/sluggishly, loiter, linger, stroll, walk
rush move/travel slowly/sluggishly
ruthless kind, gentle, merciful
sack 1. employ, engage, hire 2. protect, defend
sacred unholy, unconsecrated, unsanctified
sad happy, gay, gleeful, merry, joyful
safe 1. unsafe, insecure 2. unreliable
satisfactory unsatisfactory, inappropriate, inadequate
satisfy dissatisfy, displease, disappoint, depress, worry
saucy respectful, polite, courteous, civil
savage 1. tame, docile 2. civilized, considerate 3. calm, serene
save 1. seize, capture 2. distribute, scatter, spend 3. waste, be extravagant with
scamp 1. respectable person 2. do properly, face up to
scanty abundant, ample, plentiful, adequate
scarce abundant, plentiful, ample, sufficient
scare calm, comfort, assure, embolden
scatter 1. reap, pick, gather, collect, harvest 2. assemble, meet, congregate
scoff praise, applaud, congratulate
scold praise, commend, applaud, encourage
scorn admire, esteem, honor, respect
scrap 1. whole, total 2. retain, keep 3. become friends
scream whisper, sigh, speak softly, mutter
screen reveal, expose, show, exhibit
search 1. lose, mislay 2. find, recover
secret known, proclaimed, announced
section whole, total, all
secure 1. insecure, unsafe, unfastened, loose, unstable 2. return, replace 3. neglect
see 1. ignore, disregard 2. misunderstand
seize release, deliver, return
seldom often, frequently, on many occasions
select reject, refuse, decline, return
sell buy, purchase
send 1. retain, keep, withhold 2. return
senseless 1. sensible, wise 2. conscious, aware
sensible 1. senseless, foolish, stupid, absurd, ridiculous, silly 2. unconscious, unaware
separate undivided, connected, attached, together, joined, united
serene disturbed, ruffled, upset, excited
serious 1. frivolous, comic 2. happy, merry, gay 3. unimportant, trivial
set 1. displace, remove, uproot 2. soften, melt
settle 1. rise, ascend, fly off 2. disarrange
sever join, unite
severe 1. soft, easy, gentle, flexible 2. elaborate, sophisticated 3. mild, calm
shabby 1. well-dressed, smart, neat, tidy 2. kind, sympathetic, considerate
shady 1. bright, well-lit, sunny 2. honest, trustworthy
shake keep/remain still/rigid, freeze
sham real, true, genuine, authentic
shame honor, respect, praise, commend
shameless honorable, respectable, praiseworthy
shape misshape, deform, mutilate
share 1. keep, retain, withhold 2. abstain from
sharp 1. dull, blunt 2. gentle, mild, tender, insipid 3. unintelligent, slow-witted, stupid, inattentive, unwary
sheer 1. gradual, gentle 2. slight 3. thick, bulky
shelter reveal, uncover, expose, endanger
shield reveal, uncover, expose, endanger
shift remain/keep still/firm, rest
shine 1. tarnish, make/grow dull 2. dullness
shock please, delight, charm, comfort, soothe
short 1. long, lengthy, tall, extended 2. ample, abundant, plentiful, rich 3. courteous, polite
shortage abundance, sufficiency, wealth, surplus
shout whisper, speak quietly, mutter, moan
show cover, conceal, hide, mask, disguise
shred total, whole

shrewd foolish, obtuse, thoughtless, imprudent
shrill soft, faint, gentle, low-pitched
shut 1. open, unfastened, unlocked released 2. free, shy bold, impertinent, fearless, heedless
sick well, healthy, fit, sound
significant insignificant, unimportant, trivial
silent noisy, loud, rowdy, clamorous
silly sensible, sane, intelligent, wise, rational, reasonable, logical
simple 1. difficult, hard, complicated 2. elaborate, sophisticated 3. insincere, dishonest
sincere insincere, dishonest, not genuine, hypocritical
skillful unskilled, inexpert, untalented, incompetent, inefficient
slack 1. tight, taut, rigid 2. careful, diligent, quick, busy
slay preserve, protect, defend, spare
sleek dull, lusterless, coarse, drab
slender 1. wide, broad, thick 2. abundant, ample
slight 1. large, significant, important, severe 2. stout, strong, sturdy 3. praise, commend
slim 1. fat, wide 2. strong, great, good
slip correction, amendment
sly open, honest, sincere, straightforward
small big, large, significant, important
smart 1. untalented, dull, stupid, unwary 2. untidy, shabby, unfashionable 3. tender, mild, painless, easy
smooth 1. uneven, rough, coarse 2. restless, agitated
snatch return, replace, restore
sneer praise, applaud, commend, encourage
sob laugh, smile, grin, chuckle
sober gay, merry, undignified, drunk, intoxicated
soft 1. hard, solid, strong, rigid, stiff, unyielding 2. severe, harsh, strict 3. loud, high-pitched
solemn happy, gay, merry, undignified
solid 1. hollow, empty 2. soft, weak 3. unsound, unreliable
solitary 1. several, many 2. accompanied, crowded
soothe irritate, vex, annoy, disturb, agitate
sore 1. painless, insensitive 2. pleased, happy
sorrow happiness. joy, delight, comfort
sorry 1. happy, glad, delighted, pleased 2. impressive, pleasing, delightful
sound 1. quietness, silence 2. unsound, silly, foolish, ridiculous, absurd 3. unfit, unhealthy
sour 1. sweet, mild 2. cheerful, pleasant
source end, finish
space barrier, blockage, stop
spare abundant, ample, plentiful, generous
sparse ample, adequate, rank, thick
speed slowness, sluggishness, tardiness
splendid dull, inferior, unimpressive, not exciting
spoil 1. protect, preserve, retain, keep 2. thrive, flourish, grow
spread 1. gather, collect, pick/roll up 2. hide, conceal
squabble agree, concur, cooperate
squalid pleasing, pleasant, clean, lovely
start 1. stop, finish, end, terminate, conclude 2. return, go/come back
startle soothe, please, comfort, pacify
staunch disloyal, unfaithful, inconstant, unreliable
stay go, leave, depart, set off
steady unsteady, unstable, not firm, shaky
stern gentle, kind, friendly, considerate
stiff soft, limp, flaccid, movable
still 1. active, moving 2. loud, noisy
stir soothe, calm, quiet, pacify
stop 1. begin, commence, start, open 2. go, depart, return
store distribute, scatter, dispose of
story fact, truth
stout 1. thin, slender, lean, slight 2. weak, delicate, fragile 3. timid, afraid, cowardly
straight 1. bent, curved, crooked, uneven 2. untidy, incorrect 3. false, insincere, hypocritical
strange ordinary, normal, regular, familiar
strict gentle, kind, tolerant, easy-going
strong 1. weak, feeble, delicate 2. dull, dim, faint 3. fresh, pure
stubborn flexible, yielding
stupid sensible, intelligent, logical, rational
sturdy weak. feeble, delicate, frail, sickly
subdue surrender, yield, give in, submit
succeed 1. lose, fail, decline 2. precede, go before/in front

sudden slow, gradual, measured
suffer 1. avoid, overcome 2. forbid, disallow
sufficient insufficient, inadequate, not enough
suggestion command, order, instruction, directive
suitable unsuitable, improper, inappropriate, unbecoming
superb ordinary, commonplace, inferior, uninspiring
support abandon, forsake, hinder, burden
suppose know, understand, be certain/sure
sure unsure, uncertain, indefinite, doubtful
surly pleasant, agreeable, genial, friendly
surprise expectation, anticipation
surrender conquer, defeat, beat, subdue, suppress
suspicious certain, sure, trustworthy, reliable
sweet sour, bitter, acid, tart, malodorous, displeasing, disagreeable, unpleasant, obnoxious
swift slow, sluggish, gradual, tardy
sympathy disinterest, indifference, coldness
system disorder, confusion, mess, chaos
tactful tactless, indiscreet, undiplomatic, blundering
taint preserve, keep, clean, purify
take give, offer, present, donate, return, release
tale fact, truth
talent inability, incapability, incompetence
talkative silent, quiet, uncommunicative, taciturn
tall short, low, slight, squat
tame wild, savage, fierce, not domesticated
tasteful displeasing, inartistic, unstylish, inelegant
tasty tasteless, unsavory, bitter, tart, insipid
teach learn, study
tease please, charm, soothe, placate, pacify
tedious interesting, exciting, amusing, entertaining, appealing
tempt repel, disenchant, disillusion
tender 1. hard, rough, coarse, tough 2. harsh, unkind, unsympathetic 3. painless, easy
terminate begin, start, commence, open
terrible pleasing, pleasant, charming, attractive
terrific small, trifling, unimportant, insignificant
terrified calm, assured, serene, composed
terror courage, boldness, unconcern, indifference
thankful unthankful, ungrateful, thankless, unrewarding
thick 1. sparse, scanty, meager 2. thin, narrow, slender, slim, slight
thin 1. fat, stout, thick, wide, broad 2. sufficient, adequate, abundant, ample
think disbelieve
thorough incomplete, unsatisfactory, imperfect,
threaten placate, mollify, pacify, console
throw catch, hold, grab, snatch, trap
tidy untidy, disorderly, messy
tight loose, insecure, weak, elastic
timid bold, daring, brazen, brave
tiny big, large, great, huge, significant
tire refresh, invigorate, beguile, excite
tiresome refreshing, invigorating, stimulating, inspiring
toil ease, rest, relaxation, leisure
tolerate forbid, prohibit, disallow, ban
top bottom, base, foundation
torment please, comfort, ease, pacify
tough soft, weak, feeble, delicate, frail
tow push, shove, drive
trace lose, mislay, drop, conceal, hide
tragic comic, funny, amusing, happy
trained uneducated, unprepared
tranquil disturbed, bothered, noisy, violent
transform preserve, keep, maintain, retain
trap release, set free, liberate, rescue
treachery honesty, loyalty, faithfulness, trustworthiness, constancy
treat displease, upset, bother
tremble keep still/steady, be petrified
tremendous small, tiny, minute, insignificant
trick 1. enlighten, inform 2. be honest with
tricky 1. honest, open 2. easy, straightforward
triumph defeat, failure, loss
trivial significant, important, outstanding
trouble calm, quiet, pacify, console
true 1. untrue, false, bogus, counterfeit 2. unfaithful, disloyal, insincere
trust distrust, disbelief, doubt, suspicion
trustworthy unreliable, unfaithful, disloyal, dishonest, treacherous
truth untruth, dishonesty, fabrication, fiction, lie, falsehood

try give up, lose heart, neglect
ugly 1. beautiful, handsome, lovely, attractive 2. pleasant, safe
unable able, capable, empowered
unaware aware, alert, conscious, awake
uncertain certain, sure, definite, settled
uncivil civil, courteous, polite, respectful
unclean clean, untainted, unsullied, pure
uncomfortable comfortable, agreeable, easy, pleasing
uncommon common, ordinary, usual, regular
unconcerned concerned, bothered, worried, troubled
uncouth graceful, refined, elegant, courteous
uncover cover, hide, disguise, mask
undecided decided, certain, sure, arranged
underhand honest, truthful, sincere, straightforward
understand misunderstand, not grasp/realize/perceive/comprehend
undeserved deserved, merited, earned
undiscovered discovered, found, revealed, disclosed
undisturbed disturbed, troubled, unsure, ruffled
undoubted doubtful, uncertain, unsure, deniable
unearth lose, mislay, conceal, hide
uneasy easy, comfortable, calm, serene
unequal equal, identical, equivalent, even
unequalled equalled, matched, surpassed, exceeded
uneven even, level, flat, straight, uniform
unexpected expected, anticipated, foreseen, prophesied
unfair fair, just, proper, impartial
unfaithful faithful, loyal, true, devoted
unfasten fasten, tie, bind, connect, unite
unfit 1. fit, suitable, appropriate 2. well, healthy
unfortunate fortunate, lucky, successful
unfriendly friendly, companionable, genial, sociable
ungrateful grateful, thankful, appreciative, obliged
unhappy happy, glad, contented, uplifted
uniform unequal, uneven, irregular, varied
unimportant important, great, famous, significant
unjust just, fair, impartial, proper, apt
unkind kind, sympathetic, considerate, generous
unknown known, understood, discovered
unlikely likely, probable, possible
unlucky lucky, fortunate, successful
unnecessary necessary, wanted, needed, required
unreasonable reasonable, sensible, logical, sane
unreliable reliable, dependable, trustworthy
unruly orderly, disciplined, obedient
unsatisfactory satisfactory, suitable, appropriate, pleasing
unskilled skilled, talented, expert, trained
untidy tidy, neat, trim, orderly
until from when, from the time when
untrue 1. true, correct, right, accurate 2. loyal, faithful, constant
unusual usual, ordinary, common, normal
unwise wise, sagacious, sensible, prudent
unworthy worthy, worthwhile, deserving, honorable
upright 1. flat, level, horizontal 2. dishonest
uproar quiet, peace, calm, order
upset 1. set, place, plant 2. console, please
urge discourage, dissuade, deter
urgent unimportant, trivial, insignificant
use 1. misuse, waste, maltreat 2. keep, retain
useful useless, pointless, futile, unhelpful
useless useful, helpful, profitable, effective
usual unusual, uncommon, rare, irregular
utmost nearest, closest, smallest, weakest
uttermost nearest, closest, smallest, weakest
vacant 1. filled, taken, occupied, reserved 2. alert, wide-awake, sensible, shrewd
vacate fill, occupy, return to
vagabond upright/respectable person, hero, saint
vague clear, distinct, plain, certain, sure, definite, unambiguous
vain 1. humble, meek, simple, shy, unpretentious 2. useful, purposeful, meaningful, sensible
valiant ungallant, afraid, cowardly, unheroic
valley hill, mount, mound, mountain
value unimportance, insignificance, demerit
vanish appear, become visible, materialize
vanquish surrender, submit, yield, give in
variety sameness, similarity
various few, not many
vast small, tiny, minute, miniature, insignificant
vend purchase, buy
verbal not spoken, written
versatile rigid, inflexible, limited
vertical flat, level, horizontal

vex soothe, console, please, pacify
vice virtue, morality, decency, goodness, respectability, rectitude
vicious virtuous, moral, chaste, decent, good, respectable, rightful, kind, considerate
victim slayer, pursuer, hunter, predator
victory defeat, failure, loss
view 1. indifference, lack of interest disregard 2. ignore, disregard
vigilant inattentive, unaware, incautious, unwary
vigorous weak, feeble, lifeless, dispirited, inactive,
vile good, moral, virtuous, righteous, noble, saintly, pure, worthy
villain good/moral/upright person, hero, saint
violate 1. protect, preserve, defend, respect, improve 2. obey, observe
violent gentle, calm, peaceful, peaceable
virile weak, inactive, unhealthy, unmanly
virtue vice, wickedness, evil, immorality, wrongdoing, sin, corruption, defect, blemish
visible invisible, unseen, indiscernible, unclear
vision 1. reality 2. lack of imagination/ foresight/forethought
vital unnecessary, unimportant, trivial, inessential
vivacious dull, inactive, lifeless, torpid
vivid dull, faint, feeble, colorless, drab
vocal unspoken, not voiced/said
void 1. full, occupied, useful, valid, binding 2. receive, accept, ingest
volunteer decline, refuse, deny
vouch deny, gainsay
vulgar refined, cultured, courteous, polite, dignified, well-bred
vulnerable invincible, unassailable, safe, secure
wait go, depart, leave, retire, quit
wander 1. remain, stay 2. keep to the point
wane wax, flow, increase, rise, strengthen
want abundance, plenty, wealth, prosperity, affluence
warn praise, applaud, commend
warp straighten, unbend, preserve, keep
wary incautious, unwise, unwary, imprudent
waste 1. care, economy, thrift 2. grow, flourish, wax 3. finished article, product
wasteful careful, economical, thrifty, provident
watch ignore, disregard, neglect, be unwary/ inattentive
waver be certain/sure/steadfast, stand firm
wax wane, weaken, diminish, sink, ebb
wayward normal, obedient, amenable, dutiful
weak 1. strong, robust, powerful, firm, forceful 2. steadfast, resolute, deep
wealth need, want, poverty, destitution
weary fresh, lively, vigorous, eager
weep laugh, smile, chuckle
weird normal, regular, usual, common
wet dry, parched, scorched, arid
white 1. black, dark, swarthy 2. dirty, soiled
whole 1. incomplete, divided, partial 2. unsound
wicked 1. virtuous, sinless, moral, pious, respectable 2. good, well-behaved
wide narrow, thin, slender, slim, lean, slight
wild 1. tame, docile, domesticated, civilized 2. cultivated
willful 1. unintentional, accidental 2. easygoing, obedient, amenable
win lose, fail, give in, yield, surrender, submit
wise unwise, silly, foolish, imprudent
withdraw advance, continue, proceed, go on
withstand yield, collapse under
wonderful uninspiring, unimpressive, ordinary, commonplace, unspectacular
work 1. unemployment, inactivity, idleness, laziness 2. play, leisure
worn 1. new, fresh, unused, well-kept, well-preserved 2. refreshed, invigorated
worry soothe, please, comfort, console
worship irreverence, disrespect
worthless worthy, esteemed, valuable, useful
worthy worthless, base, ignoble, dishonest
wound protect, defend, preserve, spare
wrath calmness, composure, gentleness
wreck protect, preserve, maintain, keep
wretched 1. happy, gay, merry, bright, cheerful 2. noble, worthy, respected
wrong 1. right, correct, proper, accurate, suitable 2. virtuous, moral, righteous, just 3. legal, lawful, legitimate
yank push, shove, thrust, poke, jab
yell speak quietly/softly, murmur, moan
yield 1. defeat, conquer, subdue, vanquish, overcome 2. receive, accept

young old, aged, elderly, adult, mature, grown-up
youngster oldster, adult, grown-up, mature person
youth 1. age, maturity 2. man

zeal indifference, lack of interest, disinclination
zest torpor, dullness, sluggishness
zip indifference, feebleness, laziness

Forming Opposites

The foregoing list includes most of the antonyms that are in common use. Some of the others may be formed by using *affixes – ab-, dis-, -ful, -less, in-, un-,* etc.

An affix that is attached to the front of a word is called a *prefix:* e.g., *dis-* in *disorder.*

An affix that is attached to the end of a word is called a *suffix:* e.g., *-less* in *careless.*

These affixes, with examples to show how they are used, are listed below. However, you must be cautious when using affixes, for they can sometimes be misleading, e.g., *disorder* is an antonym of *order,* but *discipline* is not an antonym of *'cipline' – 'cipline'* is not a word. Similarly, *inconstant* is an antonym of *constant,* but *inhabit* is not an antonym of *habit,* though both *inhabit* and *habit* are words.

Prefixes

a-	moral, amoral
ab-	normal, abnormal
ant-	arctic, antarctic
anti-	climax, anticlimax
counter-	balance, counterbalance
dis-	approve, disapprove
extra-	ordinary, extraordinary
im-	possible, impossible
in-	gratitude, ingratitude
mis-	understand, misunderstand
non-	sense, nonsense
pro-	claim, proclaim
retro-	active, retroactive
un-	do, undo
under-	privileged, underprivileged

Suffixes

-ee	employer, employee
-er	drawee, drawer
-ful	careless, careful
-less	fearful, fearless

Archaic Words

Archaic means 'out-of-date,' or 'obsolescent.' Archaic words are out-of-date words, that is, words that were once in common use but which, nowadays, are either never used at all or are used only occasionally.

Some of the commoner archaic words that are still in occasional use are listed below. These words are generally encountered in poetry, both classical and modern, and stories and plays that were written several centuries ago. Archaic words abound in fables and fairy stories.

adieu	*n.*	good-bye, farewell
afar	*adv.*	at/to a distance, to a remote/distant land/place
alack	*adv.*	surprisingly, unexpectedly
ay	*n.*	yes, yea
aye	*adv.*	ever, always
bard	*n.*	poet, minstrel
betroth	*v.*	bind, promise to marry/wed
changeling	*n.*	elf-child (left by fairies)
chanticleer	*n.*	cockerel
childe	*n.*	knight, squire, page
childer	*n.*	children
cubit	*n.*	forearm-length, 50 centimeters
dam	*n.*	mother
dexter	*a.*	of/on the right-hand side
dost	*v.*	do
doth	*v.*	does
erstwhile	*adv.*	formerly
eve	*n.*	evening
farthing	*n.*	quarter of a penny
fealty	*n.*	duty, loyalty, obligation
gobbet	*n.*	piece, morsel, lump
goodly	*a.*	1. handsome, comely 2. gallant 3. large
gramophone	*n.*	record player
grist	*n.*	corn, malt
groat	*n.*	fourpenny piece/coin
hand	*n.*	10 centimeters
hither	*adv.*	here, to this place, in this direction
howbeit	*adv.*	nevertheless, for all that
joust	*n.*	just, knightly combat
lackaday	*adv.*	grievously, sadly
lea	*n.*	meadow, grassland
league	*n.*	about five kilometers
leech	*n.*	physician, doctor
lilliputian	*a.*	small, little, miniature
linden	*n.*	lime, lime tree
lo	*int.*	look, see, behold
marconigram	*n.*	telegram
methinks		I think. It seems to me.
morn	*n.*	morning
nay	*adv.*	no, not
oft	*adv.*	often, frequently
peradventure	*adv.*	perhaps, if, lest
perchance	*adv.*	maybe, possibly
physic	*n.*	medicine
pied	*a.*	multicolored, variegated
plenteous	*a.*	plentiful, abundant, ample
Reynard	*n.*	fox
russet	*a.*	1. reddish-brown 2. rustic, homely
sinister	*a.*	of/on the left-hand side
sire	*n.*	father
sirrah	*n.*	sir
swain	*n.*	lover, suitor (male)
thee	*pron.*	you
thine	*pron.*	yours
thither	*adv.*	there, yonder, to that place
thou	*pron.*	you
thy	*a.*	your
tidings	*n.*	news, information
trice	*n.*	moment, second
troth	*n.*	truth, honesty, constancy
tryst	*n.*	meeting, appointment
twain	*n.*	two
welladay	*adv.*	grievously, sadly
whatso	*a.*	whatsoever, whatever
whither	*adv.*	where, to what place
wilt	*v.*	will
wireless	*n.*	radio
without	*conj.*	unless
	adv.	outside
ye	*pron.*	you
yea	*n.*	yes, ay
yon	*a.*	yonder, distant

Foreign Words and Phrases

Many English words are of foreign origin. For example: *spirit, spiritus (Latin); jealous, jaloux (French).* Many of the foreign words and phrases listed below are in common use but have not yet been fully accepted into the English language. They are usually printed in italics.

Abbreviations used: *Arab.* Arabic, *Chin.* Chinese, *Fr.* French, *Gael.* Gaelic (Scottish or Irish), *Ger.* German, *Gk.* Greek, *Hind.* Hindustani, *It.* Italian, *Lat.* Latin, *Sp.* Spanish, *f.* feminine, *m.* masculine.

ad hoc (Lat.) special, immediate, for a particular occasion

ad infinitum (Lat.) indefinitely, eternally

ad interim (Lat.) for the time being

ad libitum (Lat.) freely, without restraint, ad lib

affaire de coeur (Fr.) love affair, romance

aide-de-camp (Fr.) assistant, deputy

à la carte (Fr.) as per the menu

alma mater (Lat.) his/her/their old college

amour propre (Fr.) pride, vanity, dignity

ancien régime (Fr.) old order/former government

anno Domini (Lat.) the year of Our Lord, A.D.

ante meridiem (Lat.) before noon

au fait (Fr.) acquainted, knowledgeable

auf Wiedersehen (Ger.) goodbye, farewell

au pair (Fr.) mutual service

au revoir (Fr.) goodbye, farewell

badinage (Fr.) banter, raillery, chaffing

belles lettres (Fr.) literary writings/studies

bête noire (Fr.) pet dislike/aversion

billet-doux (Fr.) love letter

Blitzkrieg (Ger.) violent war/campaign

bona fide (Lat.) in good faith

bon-bon (Fr.) sweet, confection

bon mot (Fr.) witty remark/comment

bon voyage (Fr.) pleasant/safe journey

camaraderie (Fr.) comradeship

carte blanche (Fr.) freedom of action, free hand

char (Chin.) tea

chic (Fr.) smart, elegant, dainty

circa (Lat.) about (dates)

communiqué (Fr.) official message/bulletin

confrère (Fr.) confidant

cul-de-sac (Fr.) blind alley/road

cum (Lat.) with

débâcle (Fr.) downfall, collapse

début (Fr.) first appearance

décor (Fr.) system of decoration

Deo volente (Lat.) God willing

de rigueur (Fr.) as demanded by etiquette

de trop (Fr.) too much, superfluous

dhobi (Hind.) washerman, washerwoman

émigré (Fr.) political exile

en bloc (Fr.) all together, in one body

encore (Fr.) again, repeat, repetition

en masse (Fr.) all together, in one mass

en passant (Fr.) ii, passing, by-the-by

en route (Fr.) on the way

ennui (Fr.) boredom, disinterest

entrée (Fr.) 1. right to be admitted
2. first course (meals)

entre nous (Fr.) between ourselves, confidentially

ersatz (Ger.) substitute, artificial, synthetic

esprit de corps (Fr.) team spirit, cooperation

exempli gratia (Lat.) for example, e.g.

exeunt (Lat.) they go out

exit (Lat.) he/she goes out

fait accompli (Fr.) accomplished feat/deed

faux pas (Fr.) blunder, error

fiancé (Fr.) m. engaged man (marriage)

fiancée (Fr.) f. engaged woman (marriage)

finis (Lat.) the end

Führer (Fuehrer) (Ger.) leader

garçon (Fr.) boy, waiter, servant

gendarme (Fr.) policeman

hoi polloi (Gk.) the common people, plebeians

hors de combat (Fr.) out of the fight, disabled

hors-d'oeuvre (Fr.) relish, extra/savory dish

id est (Lat.) that is, i.e.

ilk (Gael.) family, kin, creed

kaput (Ger.) completely finished, destroyed

kismet (Arab.) fate, fortune, destiny

kudos (Gk.) fame, glory, recognition

mot juste (Fr.) the very/apt word

ne plus ultra (Lat.) first-rate, excellent

nom de plume (Fr.) pen-name, pseudonym

non compos mentis (Lat.) of unsound mind, insane

nota bene (Lat.) note well, N.B.

par excellence (Fr.) excellently, preeminently

pâté (Fr.) paste

patois (Fr.) dialect

poilu (Fr.) French soldier

post meridiem (Lat.) after noon

presto (It.) quick, quickly, suddenly

purée (Fr.) pulp

raconteur (Fr.) storyteller, narrator

réspondez s'il vous plait (Fr.) please reply

sang-froid (Fr.) calm, coolness, composure

Sassenach (Gael.) Saxon, Englishman

savoir-faire (Fr.) tact, diplomacy, discretion

siesta (Sp.) afternoon nap/sleep

tempus fugit (Lat.) time flies/passes quickly

terra frima (Lat.) firm ground, solid earth

tête-à-tête (Fr.) face to face, secretively

videlicet (Lat.) namely, that is to say, viz.

volte-face (Fr.) sudden reversal of opinion/attitude

Weltpolitik (Ger.) world/international politics